Adora: My Hell. My Hope

God bless you!

Thanks for the
words of love,

love,

Davida Porter

ADORA: My Hell, My Hope by Daniela Potra

ISBN-13: 9781733174749
ISBN-10: 1733174745

Edited by Rachel Newman
Cover Design by Rachel Newman and Tyler Frick

Commissioned by The King's Company
Odessa, Texas, USA

Published by Lazarus Tribe Media, LLC
Rome, Georgia, USA
www.lazarustribe.media

Printed in the United States of America

Adora

my hell, my hope

BY DANIELA POTRA

THE KING'S COMPANY
ODESSA, TEXAS

Lazarus Tribe Media
Rome, Georgia

In loving memory of my beautiful mother who found herself swept off her feet suddenly on her birthday last year to celebrate with the One she loved the most! Her warm and caring heart lives on in my heart and mind. I will forever cherish her and her legacy of love!

TABLE OF CONTENTS

FOREWORD

When I first met Daniela, she immediately seemed the type who is seldom fazed by life, one who rarely gets angry, someone who has it all together, and has the happy, wholesome, girl-next-door persona.

In the pages of this book, she openly details the depths of desperation, despondency, despair, and hopelessness that she personally went through – for years!

From Daniela's raw and real recounting of several childhood traumas, to the deep and dark depression she plunged into during her adult years... From the unfailing and unconditional love she received from her parents, to the many occasions wherein ending her life seemed to be her only option...

...she gently weaves a tapestry of her profoundly personal, undiluted stories to bring you the painful reality of what a whopping 1.4 million people annually in the United States feel, think, and go through – every single day, when they deem suicide their most viable option.

If you want a fluffy, feel-good, fantasy novel, look elsewhere.

Now, if you want an insider's perspective into what thought patterns, behavior, and intense emotional pain someone you know could be suffering through at this very moment as a result of trauma, then I invite you to read and learn from this book.

If you want to experience **real** hope, if you want to know that there is a way out, then do pore through the pages of this book.

I also encourage you to buy another copy for the mother whose child has been bullied and has begun cutting, or for the father whose increasingly reclusive son, unbeknownst to the family, has been molested by a "trustworthy" family friend.

Daniela's story is ultimately a story of breakthroughs and miracles, a story of undying hope, unswerving faith – especially that of her parents, and the power of GOD's unfailing love, which can reach and transform even the most despondent person whose heart has been wounded, shattered, and ravaged by the enemy of our souls.

She truly understands. And Daniela can help you discover a way out.

Jackie Morey
Multiple-time #1 International Bestselling Author
Business Strategist
Book Writing and Publishing Coach
Prophetic Mentor
Host of "The Exponential You" podcast

PREFACE

Content warning: Words are powerful. Some words heal and encourage, but some words hurt and tear down. Words can trigger undesirable thoughts or feelings that may affect you to the core of your being. If you find yourself being tempted to act on such feelings, I would strongly caution you to put the book down and take a break from reading. You may want to talk about what you are feeling with a trusted friend, a mentor, or a counselor. When you read my story, you will read about some very dark times, but, fear not, as you keep reading, you will see that there is light at the end of the tunnel. Some of the content in the book involves aspects and struggles related to sexuality as well. If you are a parent, you may want to read the book first and decide if it is appropriate for your child to read at this time.

PART ONE

1

THE WAR IS ON

I am Adora Hopley. Before I tell you my own life story, I must talk about my mother's journey as it seems to me there's been a war throughout my bloodline. On the women's side there has been an assignment to destroy us physically, emotionally, spiritually, and in other aspects of life. My mother, myself, and my daughter, all survived some sort of near-death experience in our young lives. Coincidence? Maybe, but I'll let you draw your own conclusions.

My mother, Ella, was born in 1947 in Romania. She was the only girl in her family, the baby sister. Her two brothers were entrusted with babysitting her now and then while their mother did chores around the house. One day, when she was just over a year old, her brothers looked out for her in their father's shop. During play, the boys set her on their father's tall work table. She would throw things down from there and the brothers retrieved them. That

was a fun little game for a while, but then she decided to
bend over and look as one brother picked up whatever she
dropped. She leaned, fell off the table, hit a metal bar, and
tragically fractured her spine. Three of her lumbar verte-
brae fractured in the fall and she became paralyzed from
the waist down.

Little Ella became "the little cripple." She had to wear a
body cast for five years. Much of her time was spent alone
in her bed. She would watch longingly from her window
as her brothers, her cousins, and their friends played together in the yard.

Ella was in and out of the hospital to get her casts
changed as she outgrew them. She described her experience,

> "Every cast change was a horror for
> me. They put me on my tummy on an
> operating table, put a lot of padding
> on me and applied plaster all over. I
> had to lie in that position until the cast
> hardened. Mama cried more than I did.
> After the cast dried my mother took
> me home on the train. She had to walk
> 7 kilometers (4.3 miles) from the train
> station to our home, carrying me in her
> arms. When I was 4 years old, my left
> leg became infected with Tuberculosis
> and swelled up badly. Mama took me
> out of the cast and kept me on a grain-
> filled sack that molded to my body
> and kept it in alignment. The doctors
> from the hospital were pleased with
> her idea, and it was more comfortable
> than the cast."

Since antibiotic treatment for TB was not available in
Romania in 1950, Ella was sent home from the hospital for
the time being. The doctors from the Cluj hospital told Ella's mother they would have to amputate her left leg.

Here's how my mom remembered it:

> "One day Mom put me in a special-
> ly designed bathtub, filled with medic-
> inal herbal tea for my daily bath. The

skin cracked, the water became white
like milk, and the bone that looked
partially disintegrated came out in
small pieces. One of the doctors from
the hospital came to our home, collect-
ed the bone pieces for a lab study, and
told my Mom to take me back to the
hospital for amputation. She did, and a
few days later, the infection moved to
my right leg which swelled up, cracked
open, and the bone drained out like
the left one. While I was at the hospital, the infection took over my whole
body. I stopped eating and drinking
and went into a coma. The doctor decided not to amputate. I was expected
to die, so I was sent home.

My parents heard that antibiotics
for TB were available in the United
States. They tried desperately to contact someone who could order some,
but their attempts failed. A doctor
from another village claimed he had
gotten a shipment of antibiotics, and
said that he could come weekly to give
me an antibiotic injection. My parents
sold their cow and all they could sell to
pay this doctor. They tried to help me,
but they didn't know it at the time that
it wasn't antibiotics the "good doctor"
was injecting."

When it appeared that Ella would die despite all the
efforts, her dad came home from the school of theology in
Bucharest, bought her a coffin and a burial dress, and they
started to make preparations for her funeral. They thought
she would die, and would be buried before he had to go
back and take his finals for the semester.

Two weeks later, little Ella was still hanging on to life
by a tiny thread. It was hard to tell she was still breathing. Her mom would put a feather under her nose to see if
there was any air movement. Her father finally decided he
would go back to Bucharest, take his finals, and then come

back to bury her.

After about a month of going without food or fluids, when her mother thought Ella was about to die, she cried out to God in desperation. She had been reading Charles Spurgeon's sermons, which were mailed to her house monthly. She read how Jesus healed the sick and she read testimonies of how God healed people still. She read a quote from Mark 7:25 where a woman asked Jesus to heal her daughter. She started to cry, pointing to that passage in the magazine and prayed, "Lord, I am worse than a dog, but You healed that woman's daughter, You can heal my daughter too. Have mercy on me!" She could not bear to see her baby die.

To her surprise and joy, instead of slipping away into eternity, Ella opened her eyes and asked for plums. She would not have the ones her mother had put in jars for the winter. She wanted fresh plums from the plum trees. It was winter time, and snow covered the ground and the trees. A lady from church heard of the dilemma and hurried home to search around her tree to see if she could find any plums left under the leaves. She returned quickly with some wrinkled, frozen plums. She cleaned them the best she could and brought them to little Ella. "This is all I could find," she said. Ella took a couple of bites, then she settled for the preserves. She started eating and drinking and getting stronger. Soon she noticed she could even feel and move her toes. This was a real miracle as she had been a paraplegic for years. No one ever dreamed she would ever walk again.

Ella went back to the hospital for treatment and rehabilitation, and everyone was amazed at her miraculous recovery. The hospital staff asked her mother many questions about what she did and how this turn of events came about. She told them everything. She told them how she cried out to God, and she told them about the doctor that came weekly to give her shots after she was sent home from the hospital to die. Mama happened to find a vial while she was cleaning house, and gave it to the visiting nurse who came to check on Ella's progress after she was released from the hospital. It was one of the medication vials the doctor had forgotten to discard. The vial had some leftover fluid in it, and the nurse decided to take it back to the hospital for testing. The tests showed the vial had no antibiotics in it at all. Ella had been given intramuscular vitamins. The doctor was investigated, arrested, and they never saw him again. They never got their money back, either. But they had their little girl, and they were ever so grateful. It took some time, but the bones eventually grew back in her legs and hips, though she still had some impressive scars.

My mother recalled,

> "It took a long time for the bones to grow back, from 1952 to 1954. First soft cartilage grew, then it hardened and became normal bone. Those two years were so lonely, no one let their kids visit me for fear of infection. My cousins came, but they were not allowed to come in the house. They played outside, and I watched them out the window. I cried as I watched them run and play. My brothers played with me, but I wanted to play with kids my age. Sometimes they snuck in to see me; that made me feel better. It was a hard, emotional time for me".

Ella was not well enough to go to school in first grade. The teacher would come to their house after school hours to teach her and give her homework. Ella would do the schoolwork with the help of her mother and brothers. In second grade, she was carried to school by her brothers or her parents. The brothers came to detest this chore. They would sit her down at her desk at school and come to pick her up after school. She enjoyed learning, but was often ridiculed by the other kids. Her parents would encourage her at home, would pray with her, and would teach her how to cope. My mom still remembered being called "the little-crippled girl," and how she felt so bad and often cried. But she pushed through.

Little by little, Ella gained more and more strength and at age nine she started to walk. While she never got strong enough to run, she was able to lead a fairly normal life after that. At least it appeared that way to those around her.

While she was crippled and unable to walk, she spent

much of her time reading, drawing, writing, and studying. She enjoyed learning and pursued academics with excellence. When she finished high school, she was accepted into the nursing school in the city where she completed a degree. She eventually got married, and besides becoming a mother of five, she also became quite accomplished in her career and worked as a surgical nurse for 20 years before our family moved to the United States in 1985.

I still remember watching a surgery through the little window in the nurse's room. Mom was squeezing the oxygen bag to give the patient artificial respirations while the doctor was taking out the gallbladder and dissecting a part of the liver. After the surgery, my mother brought the tray and showed me the organs, blood and all. That was one of my first introductions to the surgical field.

At the beginning of this chapter, I said I noticed a trend in my family line, so before I describe my near-death experience in the next chapter, I want to share my daughter's experience when she was almost a year old.

In 2015, just as the school year started for the boys, my little girl ended up needing aggressive medial intervention after she ingested Tiki torch fuel from an open bottle that was left behind the massive floor lamp in our living room. I had left her in the living room briefly so I could get her bottle ready in the kitchen. When I came back, Zayna was waddling toward me, coughing and breathing heavily. She had an expression of disgust on her face and her eyes were watering. I noticed the open bottle behind her right away, and instinctively knew I had to call 911. The medics responded quickly, placed her on oxygen, and drove her to the hospital. I followed in my car.

When they got to the emergency room, Zayna's breathing was becoming more and more difficult as her airway swelled. The doctor placed a tube down her throat to keep her airway open. She was sedated immediately through an IV that had to be drilled into her leg bone. "This is the fastest way we can get access to deliver medications right now," the doctor explained. I knew that, but it was so hard to see that procedure being done on my own little girl.

The doctor then decided the staff at Children's Hospital in Seattle was better prepared to take care of Zayna, and she was transferred within the hour. I followed the ambulance again. I spent the next 24 hours beside the hospital crib where my little girl was lying hooked up to monitors and IV's. I held her hands, wishing I could cuddle her and hold her close. Thankfully, by the next evening the swelling subsided and the doctors were able to take the tube out of her throat. I was allowed to hold her again, and Zayna clung to me for the next week, day and night. I felt such relief being able to hold her in my arms.

Zayna developed a touch of pneumonia after that, and she had to stay in the hospital for antibiotic treatments until she was able to start taking food and fluids again. A week later she finally recovered, and we were able to come home.

I'm so grateful for family and friends who prayed and sent warm wishes and stuffed animals, cleaned our house, and helped care for our boys while Zayna recovered in the hospital. Oh, and I shouldn't forget about the teachers at school and the neighbors that helped bring our newly acquired cat, Lola, back home every time she ventured into the streets or followed the kids to school.

Though my family has experienced this trend, I believe God is giving me and my descendants tools to help prevent from perpetuating. I am grateful to look back and see the goodness of God in healing and restoring us through all the troubles.

My mom also felt that her sufferings were not in vain, and was happy to share and encourage others to believe that miracles still happen. She wrote,

> "One day, I was feeling down and having a-pity party. I started to complain to God about my condition, about the pain and suffering I've experienced all my life, about the physical scars all over my body, and the emotional scars, too. When I was done complaining, I felt like Jesus spoke to me saying? 'You have scars? I do too. Your scars were not your fault, it's true. My scars were not My fault either, but man's sin caused them, including yours. You are embarrassed and ashamed of your scars, but those

scars are proof that by My wounds you are healed.' I gave your life back to you when the casket was made ready for you, and after a new "shroud" was made for your burial. I am Jesus, and I am not ashamed of My scars. Your scars are blessed, too, showing My love for you. You can help others that are wounded to heal. Many people do not believe in miracles, but you can prove it by your scars.' I promised Jesus that I would use my scars to help others, and I wouldn't complain about them anymore."

2

TOO YOUNG TO DIE

Now that I have described a bit about my mother and my baby girl, I want to share about how I died and came back to life. In 1970, when I was only three months old, I became very ill. I had a high fever, difficulty breathing, and later started having convulsions. My father had not yet seen me. He had been drafted by the Romanian army and was stationed far away. My father asked his superiors to release him for a home visit, but the Romanian army denied his request.

My mother took me to the village clinic. The doctor was not at the clinic that day, but the nurse saw me and got me started on antibiotics and sent me home. That night after doing the best she could to get the fever down and help me to sleep, Mom fell asleep herself. We were staying with Mom's parents at the time. Mom woke up in the middle of the night and found me blue, pulseless, and breathless. She started CPR and tried to resuscitate me again and again, but there was no response. She would lay me down on the bed to check for a pulse and listen for any signs of breathing, then she would pick me up and start CPR again. She kept trying and trying, and when she did not get any results she started crying and screaming hysterically.

My grandparents, who were sleeping in the next room, woke up hearing my mother's wailing. Grandpa Papó knelt down by the bed, lay his hand on me and started to pray something like, "Dear God, You know how much we love Adora. Please give her back to us so we can enjoy her and see her grow. We are asking this in the Name of Jesus, Amen." After a few seconds, my mother tells me I started to sneeze, and after a few sneezes my breathing returned, my color returned, and I was revived. My mother estimated that I was clinically dead for at least 20 minutes, though she said it felt more like an hour. She was overjoyed with my recovery.

However, Papó was gripped by a terrifying thought. An eerie feeling came over him like there was some kind of evil presence in the room. He said to my mother and grandmother, "What have I done? What if God wanted her to go, to protect her from some terrible thing she would have to endure here on earth?"

Grandpa knelt again and started praying. "Please forgive me, Lord, if I made a mistake in asking to bring Adora back if You wanted to keep her from some terrible thing." Then he flipped through the pages of the Bible and his eyes landed on a passage from Luke 22: 31-32, "Simon, Simon, Satan has asked to sift all of you as wheat. But I have prayed for you, Simon, that your faith may not fail. And when you have turned back, strengthen your brothers." After my grandfather read that passage he was relieved, and experienced a sense of peace and calm right away.

The next day my mother took me to the doctor's office in the village. The nurse reported that she saw me for fever and respiratory distress the day before at the clinic, but when the doctor examined me, he said in amazement, "This baby was never sick."

I am glad God brought me back to life then, but as I have experienced some really dark times over the years, there have been many times I wished I had died that day. I could not figure out why God let me live, knowing full well the things that would happen to me that would lead to times of inexpressible despair. Yet at the same time, the fact that God did bring me back to life when I was a baby gave me a glimmer of hope to hold on to in the darkest days of my life. Somehow I kept thinking that maybe God would make a way, even though it seemed like that was an impossibility at the time.

3

Early in Life

I was born and grew up in Zalau, a neat little town in Romania. It's located in the northwestern region of Transilvania, about an hour's drive from Cluj. I am my parent's second child, in a family of five. I was strong-willed and stubborn. I got into trouble pretty regularly. If I wasn't fighting with my brother and my sister, I would fight with the kids in kindergarten.

In my grade school years, I remember starting each new school year with new goals of being good and having good grades. I loved the smell of my new leather backpack and the fancy new pencil boxes my mom procured. But as the year progressed, I would always find some way to get into trouble and bring shame upon myself. I never really liked to do my homework and I would frequently miss turning in assignments. One time I was labeled a "tomboy" by my grade school teacher because I played with the boys at recess and came back to class late.

Mom and Dad both worked long hours, and our grandmother on mother's side would care for us when we came home from school. We would go to church a couple of weeknights and attended the Sunday morning and evening services. It was a long walk to church, but we never complained; it was just what we did as a family. When we were not at school or at church, my siblings and I played outside with the kids from around the block.

Mom and Dad were active leaders in the church. Mom taught Sunday school, and Dad started a little orchestra. As we learned to play instruments, we all contributed to writing the songs in the notebooks and teaching the instruments to the kids at church. We also sang in the choir and with a smaller group Mom and Dad organized. Church friends would come to our house almost weekly to practice the songs, and then we would sing them in church.

With the small singing group, we were invited to sing at weddings and events in different villages and towns. It was nice to travel with our family and the little group, either in cars or by train or bus. Holidays were fun, too, especially Christmas. We enjoyed going caroling and getting treats and money from the different families we visited. There was a sense of excitement and adventure.

In 1980 we moved to a newly developed area of our growing little town. There I met my best friend forever, Sonia. Her mother died that summer in a tragic accident. Their family was close in proximity to ours, and we ended up being in the same class in school, and sat next to each other through the rest of grade school. It was a big school, grades one through eight. It had three floors, and a nice big courtyard where the boys would usually play soccer after school. The courtyard overlooked a large valley which was mostly rocky terrain, and in the distance, you could see the hills sprinkled with old homes on the other side of town. We lived in a new development of apartment buildings called Dumbrava (The Meadow). Sonia lived near the school, and we lived a few apartment buildings down from her apartment building.

Sonia had to work hard before and after school. In the evenings, she would go around the block and collect leftover food to take to the pigs her dad was growing to sell. Early in the mornings before going to school, Sonia had to walk quite a distance to take the food to the pigs on the outskirts of the town. I never heard her complain, though, and we loved talking and dreaming together whenever we got a chance. We would talk about visiting each other and building a rocket together. My parents had decided to pursue immigration to the United States. We enjoyed talking about that with our friends.

In 1985, when I was fifteen, we moved to America. We lived in Anaheim, California for a couple of years, where I finished high school. The day I graduated from high school we were all packed to move to Seattle. Dad had visited a friend in Seattle and decided we should all move there. I think the scenery reminded him of Romania. He thought he could use his background in textile manufacturing to find a good job in Seattle since the weather was colder, and knitted clothing were more likely to be a hot item. We started on our way the next day.

Dad drove one car and my brother and I took turns driving behind him. Mom was with Dad, and the younger sisters were divided between our car and Dad's car. I don't remember which sisters rode in which cars; I was more focused on the excitement of driving all the way, chasing after Dad, and honking to keep him awake. When we got to Seattle and told Dad he was driving like he was falling asleep, he said he was swerving on purpose to keep us awake!

Before Dad decided to move us to Washington State, I had my heart set on going to Stanford University and studying to become a pharmacist, but after we moved that plan seemed like it would take too long. I couldn't afford to go to a university, and I was not going to qualify for a grant because I wasn't a resident. While I was in high school, I completed an evening course at a technical school and got a medical assistant certificate. With that training, I was able to get a job at Virginia Mason as a cardiology lab technician.

My parents encouraged me to pursue nursing. "You'll never be out of a job," they both agreed. I took their advice to pay my way through nursing school. All the hospitals had lists and lists of RN jobs available when I started nursing school at Bellevue Community College, so I thought I would never have trouble finding work as a nurse. I went for it.

Well, here I was. It was 1995, I had just turned 25, and I was pretty content. I felt somewhat accomplished after finishing nursing school, and I was filled with a desire to do great things. Things were going well. I had been working as a registered nurse for two years at a wonderful little hospital in Monroe, and I was one of the few graduates from my entire class who was actually employed in a hospital. To my surprise, hospitals were not hiring new grads at the time. After much job searching, a position opened up at the Monroe hospital. I went through a series of interviews, and after weeks of waiting I was chosen for the position. I couldn't ask for anything more.

Being a "good little Christian," I involved myself in numerous church activities, contributing to different causes, teaching Sunday school, conducting a children's choir and a children's orchestra. I read my Bible, prayed almost daily, and I read many books that discussed the existence of God and His purposes. I read books about many missionaries and great people of faith such as D.L. Moody, Charles Spurgeon, George Muller, Hudson Taylor, Jim and Elizabeth Elliot, and many others. The lives of these people inspired me, and I wanted to live my life in a way that would make a difference in this world and would please God.

In 1992 I had become a U.S. citizen along with the rest of my family. I wanted to be a good citizen, studying the current issues, voting, and talking to others about the importance of getting involved and letting our voice be heard. I was well-read on many subjects, and enjoyed talking to people who would engage in meaningful conversations as opposed to talking about the weather.

Back in May of 1994 I took the opportunity, along with my brother Andrei and my sister Crina, to visit Romania. We visited relatives and looked for mission opportunities. We contributed to different causes. We visited a renowned Christian college, an orphanage, and the abandoned children's ward in a hospital in Oradea. I felt such compassion for the people there, and especially for the little children that were abandoned. I desired to do something to help these children. Coming back from the trip, I continued to support the people who were involved with these missions, but I wanted to go back and really get involved.

I considered a variety of mission opportunities, and

decided to apply to one of the organizations so I could go serve during the summer months. There were some questions asked in this application that triggered some childhood memories; things that I had forgotten about, but had not been dealt with completely. I didn't know how to answer the questions. The memories began to work on me and I started to feel inadequate to go and work for these missions. I decided to wait and not go anywhere. Instead, I took a course in critical care nursing in order to improve my skills and advance in my career to be able to help critically ill patients.

During this time, I was introduced to a young man by an acquaintance who thought we would make a great match. Joshua was a leader in his church in Sacramento, and seemed very caring and considerate. He was very handsome and charming, and had good taste. He had a college degree and was very intelligent. He said he was interested in a relationship with me that would lead to marriage.

I was excited since I thought he was perfect for me. We met a few times over a period of about 6 months. We talked a lot on the phone, we wrote back and forth, and things looked pretty bright. I thought, "Well, maybe God wants me to get married, and then support this man in whatever ministry he is called to serve."

Life in general, looked great and very promising. There was nothing too spectacular about it, but I had my basic needs met. My health was pretty good with the exception of this persistent neck tension and soreness that developed years after I had been involved in a car accident. I saw a chiropractor weekly, and the adjustments managed the pain for a while. I signed up for a fitness program which included cardiovascular exercise to warm up, and some aerobic exercise followed up by a good swim. I followed this program two to three times a week, and I noticed that it really helped my general sense of well-being; it helped my neck pain too.

I struggled with severe acne, as well, through my teenage years and into my early 20's. I made some good adjustments to my diet after consulting a naturopath and took some supplements he recommended. This regimen was very helpful.

So far, so good!

4

SUDDEN DEATH

So far, so good...until an overwhelming sense that something was very wrong came over me one day in July of 1995. I started having flashbacks that revealed some memories from my childhood and adolescent years. Then I had a flashback of a memory that triggered the thought that I had crossed the line of grace. Although I tried to bury these memories and not allow them to affect me by keeping busy and focusing on work, the feeling of being a complete failure returned early in October and would not go away.

At first, I felt a heaviness in my heart for days, a sense that I had committed the unpardonable sin and was going to hell. One instance that came to mind was when I had sinned willfully in a moment of inattentiveness (I will talk about that later in this book). At that moment, I had an impression that Christ was in the room, and He was turning away from me. I quickly rationalized it away, but things became different shortly after that time.

As October progressed in 1995, the heaviness on my heart became constant. I felt the sensation of an invisible hand that gripped my heart and pulled it down with a constantly increasing force. There was nothing I could do to get free from it. Any diversion or activity I engaged in to make me forget was useless and ineffective. There was an awful, dreadful feeling that accompanied that pulling in my heart. It was a feeling that my end was near, a feeling of doom, a feeling that hell was approaching, and I was being pulled into it, closer and closer.

I visited a psychiatrist and a couple of counselors. They listened and gave me advice. The Christian counselors prayed with me numerous times, but nothing relieved that awful tug. I confessed every sin I could think of and I felt some relief, which lasted only a few hours. I couldn't sleep at all and my body was experiencing some kind of shock. I would drink gallons of water and still feel thirsty. My senses became very dull. Food didn't have any taste and my appetite disappeared. My body felt like it was burning inside, yet on the surface, I felt shivering cold.

I went to see a family doctor for a complete physical. All was well physically, but the doctor said to me, "I have not seen anyone feeling more depressed than you in my whole life and practice." It so happened that this doctor was a Christian. He asked his nurse if she would come, and together they prayed for me in his office. He started me on antidepressants and scheduled me for a follow-up. I started taking the medication and tried to continue to function to the best of my ability.

I was not sleeping at all. Day and night, I continued to try to shake these feelings off and act normally. I was never the type of person to give up easily. I tried to find comfort in reading the Bible and looked for a verse that would help, but I would always remember Hebrews 10:26 (NKJV),

> *"For if we sin willfully after that we have received the knowledge of the truth, there no longer remains a sacrifice for sins, but a certain fearful expectation of judgment and fiery indignation, which will devour the adversaries."*

I kept trying to justify why that verse should not apply to me, because even though I had done wrong like any imperfect mortal, I could think of plenty of people that sinned in the same ways, yet they were not plagued like me. Still, this passage from the Bible kept haunting me. It was like I had chosen to jump to my death off a spiritual cliff; as though I had been cut off like a branch that is good only for the fire.

I found many scriptures that seemed to depict my desolate state of being; they jumped out at me when I read the Bible and condemned me. One such scripture was John 15:6, "If any man abide not in me, he is cast forth as a branch, and is withered; and men gather them, and cast them into the fire, and they are burned." Also, 1 Timothy 1:19, "So…you may fight the good fight, holding on to faith and a good conscience. Some have rejected these and so have shipwrecked their faith…." That is what seemed to be my condition. I was shipwrecked.

I forced myself to go to church for as long as I could. I tried to smile and function normally. It took much work to put on a smile; my facial muscles literally pulled themselves into a frown and I had to force myself to smile. One of my friends got engaged during this time, and I made an effort to go to her engagement party and even to her wedding. It was so extremely difficult to pretend nothing was wrong.

I went to work that last week in October and struggled to help my patients the best I could, but at the end of the week one of my patients filed a complaint with my supervisor, and I was called to meet her in her office. At that point, I told my nursing supervisor that I had to take a leave of absence because something was happening to me, something beyond my control that was preventing me from being able to provide adequate care to my patients.

Whatever else I said to my nursing supervisor, as well as my severely distressed appearance, frightened her enough that she asked me to sign a contract stating that I would not kill myself. I signed it and left on my leave of absence. Then in late October the pull on my heart became stronger and stronger. I continued to see a counselor, and worked with her for hours and hours with no relief. There was such a force tearing at my heart. The pain was so real and so deep. I felt it physically as well as emotionally.

Finally, after hours and hours of this agony, in a most dreaded moment in the middle of the night as I lay curled up in my bed, I felt as though my heart was being torn completely out of my chest by that invisible force.

There was nothing I could do to stop it.

My chest hurt so badly I thought I would have a heart attack and would be dead by the morning.

There was a dead silence inside of me, a feeling that God had turned His face and abandoned me completely. I had an impression that the fires of hell were the only destiny that was left for me. I don't think there are adequate words to describe how I felt and what I went through.

That traumatic feeling was so great that I thought my hair would turn white by the morning for sure, and I would look like the witches from the storybooks if I made it through the night. I felt like I was falling into a bottomless black hole. My body felt completely detached, my arms floating in the air, though they were still attached. I felt like an empty shell, a ghost, falling rapidly into this endless universe of darkness and emptiness.

The next morning, to my utter surprise, when I looked in the mirror my acne was completely gone and the skin on my face was like the skin of a baby. That was a chilling experience, and so ironic to me that I had beautiful skin now, but no life inside to be able to enjoy it. It felt like my hormones were dried up, and I was sure at that moment that I would never be able to have any children. It felt like something was disconnected. My neck pain cleared up, too. Maybe due to the tremendous emotional pain, my brain went numb. All I had left were the morbid thoughts of irreversible doom for the moments I had left to breathe, and a horrible pain in my chest where my heart used to be to torment me forever. I cried for days until I had no tears left. I screamed in pain.

My family could not understand. They surrounded me lovingly and tried to comfort me, to tell me that things would change, and I would feel well again. They hugged me, prayed and fasted for me, and listened to me. Nothing helped. I could not feel their love. Their words did not help, their hugs did not penetrate, and there was an invisible wall that repelled everything that was good. Life had seeped out from every cell of my body. I felt like the lights went out and there was no hope. I could no longer connect with the world around me. There was an invisible bubble around me that altered my perception of my surroundings.

I used to enjoy listening to music. As a young child, I played the piano, or sometimes the guitar. I also enjoyed singing and composing music. We were like the Von Trapp family growing up. We all played instruments and got together to make music two to three evenings a week, up until we moved to the States. My dad was a church leader and music director. He started a string orchestra at the church in Romania. When we came to the States we got involved in the orchestra at the Romanian church, and eventually started a couple of little orchestras ourselves when we moved to Washington State. As more Romanians started moving to the Seattle area, the church started to grow, and we were encouraged to use our talents and teach the younger kids music.

Now, my music tapes sounded out of tune, off key, far away.

My desire to sing and play music dried up.

I felt like there was no song in my heart.

I could not stand to listen to the music tapes. I forced myself to play songs on our electric piano for a while, hoping that the lack of feeling would not be permanent. I looked and longed for a spark of life that would give me a ray of hope.

As the days passed without relief, I gradually stopped all activities and withdrew into my room. Christmas Eve that year was the last time I went to church for a long time. I endured the church service to the end, and then I rushed to the car to avoid anyone asking questions. I stooped down in the back of Dad's van until the rest of the family was ready to go home.

Instead of joy, I was filled with shame and regret. I locked myself in the bathroom when church time rolled around again. Mom tried to talk me into going, but there was no use. She tried to force the door open. She begged for me to come out until she finally gave up and left.

1996 dawned with no change in my condition. I didn't want to be completely useless, but I couldn't stand to have anyone around me, so sometimes I would cook when everyone was at school or work or church. In an effort to help me, my mother asked if I would translate a workbook from a Christian marriage seminar into Romanian. I had suggested my parents attend the seminar a few months prior to all my trauma, because my parents were going through a hard time in their marriage. The course was very helpful for them, and they wanted to share it with me and with family and friends from Romania.

The material was very good, but I felt it was so ironic that I should be translating a workbook on marriage when there was no hope that I would ever marry. I worked on it for a while, but I stopped halfway through because I couldn't stand the content anymore.

To pass the time I played computer games such as Chess or Mines (GNOME) or watched TV. I still allowed a few people to come and talk to me from time to time, but no one was able to comfort me. Many friends would come and say, "I know how you feel, I went through a time like that in my life when I felt so discouraged and hopeless," and they would describe their time of sadness. Yet none of their stories compared to what I was experiencing.

I had plenty of sad times in my life prior to this, and I did not let that get to me. I always chose to look at things in a positive way, and learn from each experience rather than let it make me bitter and angry or hopeless. But what I was experiencing now was nothing like that. It was like a tsunami that came suddenly and left nothing but destruction in my heart. It was like an atomic bomb that uprooted and destroyed everything that had to do with life.

There was no way I could see myself picking up where I left off. There was nothing to hold on to. I have yet to find someone who can convince me that they have been there and know how I felt except for Jesus, who cried out in His hour of agony, "Father, why have you forsaken me?" Still, that thought brought me no comfort at that time, because I felt I had offended Him in such a way that He had turned away from me forever! I thought Jesus knew how I felt, but that didn't help me. He was able to take up His life again three days later but for me, there was no hope anymore; and forever?

After a while, I barricaded myself in my room and did not allow anyone, not even my parents, to come in. I call it my room, but it was actually my parent's room. My parents believed that there was no reason for their children to move out until they got married. At that time, I stopped taking phone calls and stopped looking at my mail, too. By this time, my relationship with the young man I was dating had dissolved, as well, because he could not possibly understand what I was experiencing.

I felt like cursing the day I was born. I said to myself, *I should have been left dead when I was an infant.* It didn't make any sense that I would be brought back to life just to end up dead in my soul without the tiniest bit of hope, without ever seeing any way I could go on.

I no longer had a place among the living.

I was no longer part of this world.

Yet, I continued to exist. I thought about suicide, but, what then? The thought of committing suicide was so overwhelming that it seemed like the only choice. Yet, I could not help but think that there was something worse beyond physical death for me. At this time, other than the constant feelings of fatigue and heaviness, I was physically healthy, and I could not imagine how it would be if I had to endure some horrible physical pain on top of the unimaginable loss of all that pertained to life. So, day in and day out, I fought with the thought of finishing it off.

The thought came to my mind, *Just curse God and die, you're dead anyway, why not just curse Him. He is responsible for allowing all this to happen to you. You didn't choose to be born, you did your best to please God and had every intention to be faithful to the end. Yet He allowed you to fail. He did not protect you. He is not good to you and never was. Don't you remember how as a child you were always getting into trouble? You always fell short in some way or another and never could measure up. You are a failure and are meant to be for an example to the world of what happens to someone like you. You betrayed Him like Judas and now there's nothing left but to wait for an even more painful, terrifying and dreadful hell after death.*

One day, my dad fought so hard to pull me out of my room and take me for a walk. I curled up on the floor, grabbed the leg of my bed, and would not let go. I just kept screaming; "Leave me alone! There is no use!" His heart must have been so grieved.

My parents did everything they could to help me. They brought food to my door daily, washed my linens, prayed, and asked many people to pray. They took away my knitting equipment so I wouldn't use the needles to hurt my-

39

self. They went to the doctor in my place and filled my prescriptions and brought the medications to me.

My parents took me to a couple in Portland, Oregon who had a prophetic ministry. They asked if they could pray and see if they could help. The man prayed, and said that God gave him a vision that I was going to be like Rachel getting water from my well and giving it to many thirsty people to drink. I thought to myself, *These people have no idea that my well is so shattered and dry that I couldn't squeeze one drop to drink for myself let alone comfort others. In fact, my well is pulverized, and nonexistent,* but I didn't say anything to the couple. I told my parents on the ride back, "You don't understand, I'm dead inside."

Later that month, my parents flew me to New York to see pastor David Wilkerson at Time Square Church. I had read about David Wilkerson and his ministry even as a child in Romania, and now my parents decided to take me there, hoping that they could help. The worship service started with the choir, accompanied by a jazz band. It was beautiful, but I cried in self-pity because I couldn't feel its beauty. "The senior pastor is out of town this weekend," the staff informed my parents at the end of the Sunday morning service. "You are welcome to come back for the evening service and stay in town for a couple of days until he gets back." All I could think of was that maybe I could jump from the hotel window, because nothing seemed to help. My parents were not prepared to stay longer, and we flew back the next day.

In my mind my problem had no solution, not because I didn't believe God could help, but it was clear to me by the way I felt that God had decided against me. As far as I could see, I had broken the covenant. I had insulted God. I had trampled the blood of Jesus after I received forgiveness when I believed and received Jesus as my Lord and Savior. I had grieved the Holy Spirit, and God had declared his judgment against me by removing Himself from me and removing His presence from every fiber of my being.

I didn't know what to do. I didn't know how to deal with the way I was feeling. All that was left was the pain in my chest in the place where my heart used to be, like the phantom pain that someone feels when a limb is amputated. I kept rehearsing the events of my life, the regret over the choices I had made, the "what if's" and the "why's"

and the "how could I" questions circled in my head con-
tinuously. I rehearsed in my mind every detail of my life,
looking for anything significant that had contributed to
my decline. I had turned over every situation, trying to
find justification for what I did.

There was an anger burning inside of me, mostly toward myself, at my failure to discern and avoid the temptation, my failure to guard my heart. I was angry at all
the people in my life who I felt had influenced me in the
wrong way, either by commission or omission, and I was
angry at God for letting it all happen.

5

TO BE OR NOT TO BE

Sometime in January of 1996, I took off a few times in my car and drove for hours, thinking that maybe I could drive off a cliff. I stayed in motels for days, surfing the TV channels to keep my mind off how I was feeling; getting out occasionally to get a bagel. I thought about what I could do since I could no longer function normally. I didn't want to be a burden on my family, and I couldn't see myself interacting with people again in any meaningful way. I couldn't imagine working in my present condition. There seemed to be no options for me.

Eventually, I drove back home. I couldn't bring myself to do anything. I asked my mother if she could find a psychiatric hospital where they could sedate me heavily, so I could have some relief. I tried different sleeping aids. I would take many strong prescription drugs at the same time hoping for comfort, but nothing worked.

I didn't care what I looked like anymore, I let my hair grow long and unkempt. I didn't bother to brush my teeth, or to shower daily. I didn't care what I was wearing, and I stayed mostly in my pajamas. If anyone entered my room, I pulled the covers over my head and remained there until they left.

Eventually, I moved to a room downstairs. I thought, *At least my parents could use my room for guests.* My new quarters were more like a storage room, but it had a bed in it. The room had no windows, which was all the same to me since I couldn't enjoy nature; and I hated to see people going about their business, getting on with their lives when I had no life and no hope that anything would ever get better. The only feelings I had left were feelings of anger about my condition and my inability to do anything about it, and feelings of fear of the future.

The only thing that kept me from committing suicide was the thought that even though I was in hell emotionally, the hell described in the Bible after death would be a lot worse. So eventually I decided suicide was not an option.

1996 was a terrible year. Day after day there was no sleep, no rest, no relief, and no hope; just the torment of the morbid feelings and thoughts, the struggle to understand why, and the question of what to do in my situation. When I say no sleep, I mean no sleep, not even a minute. That's how bad it was, and sleep medication did not have any effect.

It must have been May or June of 1996 when my dad had finally had enough. He broke my door down and had me committed to a hospital in a lockdown unit, where I was to spend 3 days and then go in front of a medical judge who would decide what to do with me. By this time the feelings of shock-like the constant thirst and the feelings of burning inside and cold on the outside, had subsided. All that was left was empty silence. I felt like an empty shell.

At the hospital the staff tried to talk with me, involve me in help groups and encourage me, but I just stayed withdrawn, refusing to talk about anything significant since I didn't feel anyone could help. Some of the patients talked to me, and one of the men invited me to a Chess game, the one Chess game that I won in my life. He didn't talk much. He was old, had long straggly white hair and a long beard. He had an eerie look and feel about him. Another man shared that he shot himself in the chest after his wife left him, and that's why he was there. He said he was sorry for doing such a stupid thing.

I shared a room with another girl. She was there because of some drug addiction problem. She talked to me and tried to encourage me. Most of the people I met in lockdown had something in common, as I saw it: they still had life and hope, but I didn't. I thought there was hope for them, but I didn't see or feel there was any chance for me.

Some of the staff asked me if I wanted to talk about my problems. I told them there was no use since my case was hopeless and there was nothing they could do to help. I had tried psychiatrists and counselors in outpatient settings prior to my hospitalization. I had talked for hours and hours, expressing every thought and feeling to different counselors. I had tried medication. Nothing worked!

Eventually the psychiatrist on staff asked me simply, "Do you plan to harm yourself?" I said, "No." He continued, "Do you plan to harm others?" I said, "I will leave that up to God." The psychiatrist then diagnosed me with "inorganic brain disorder," which basically told me that he really had no clue about what ailed me. I thought he got the inorganic disorder part right, but I did not think I had a brain disorder at all. My pain was in my heart and my soul, not my brain. I did not see a connection at the time.

On the third day of lockdown, the staff took me across the street to the building where a medical judge was going to see me. The nurse said the judge would ask me what I planned to do with myself. At the nurse's request, I shared what I would say to the judge. I said that I would try to function to the best of my ability, try to reintegrate into society, and see what happens. He asked, "How do you think you will accomplish that? Do you have a plan in mind?" I said, "I guess if my parents will let me come home, I could start by leaving the door open and letting people come in." After the staff spoke with my parents that morning, they decided that since I was willing to try, I did not need to see the judge, and I was released to go home with my parents.

I was sent home with a few medications. I took them, but they gave me terrible side effects. I would take Benadryl as advised, along with the new medications to try to alleviate the side effects, but it didn't help much. After a few months of that, I stopped taking the medications because I felt no relief whatsoever. I still couldn't sleep, but I learned to cope. I was sore all over and felt worn out all the time.

6

MY ACTING CAREER

Now it was the summer of 1996, and I was stuck! What could I do? I moved back to my room in my parents house upstairs and left the door open so my family could come in and visit. I began talking a little with my immediate family. I started to knit to pass the time. I allowed my youngest sister, Elena, to cut my hair. She was sixteen at the time. I think it was the first time she ever gave someone a haircut, and it didn't turn out too badly. Now she's a hairdresser, and the best in my estimation. Eventually, I asked my family to forgive me for not letting them in and for my angry outbursts towards them.

Time passed, and I started to go outside for short walks. One of my childhood friends, who had just come to visit the United States, called me and invited me to spend some time in California where he was staying with friends. I accepted his invitation and flew down. Somehow, I felt safe to share about how I was feeling.

All this time, the feelings of complete death inside persisted and I still could not sleep, but I found it a little easier to act like nothing was wrong, especially around people outside my family and close friends. With my family, I shared my feelings and continued to tell them that I still felt there was no hope for me. Sometimes I would rehash the things that happened to me in the past and blame my parents and the other people who were influences in my life for my current state of being.

I shared my feelings with my friend I visited in California. He listened and encouraged me. We took a trip to see the Grand Canyon with a few other mutual friends, and we stayed with another childhood acquaintance and his family. That night, I fell asleep for a few minutes only to be awakened by a nightmare in which a ghostly figure appeared in the far distance, and then in a flash appeared in front of me. This startled me, and I screamed at the top of my lungs. I tossed and turned the rest of the night. My shriek didn't seem to stir anyone, but the lady of the house did ask in the morning, "Which one of you had a nightmare last night?" I admitted it was me. She smiled and that was that.

The visit with my friend proved to me that I could act like things were okay for the most part, and so I ventured out to get a job. I talked with my nursing supervisor at the hospital in Monroe where I had worked previously and asked her if there was a possibility of working there again. She said she could not rehire me as I had not communicated with her for a whole year after my leave, but she wished me the best with my job search. I started looking at other possibilities. In the meantime, I started working for an agency that would send nurses to different nursing homes that were short-staffed, and I would work either as a charge nurse or a med nurse, depending on the need.

And so began my "acting career," acting like everything was fine as I went to work every day. It was extremely difficult at first because I thought people could see right through me. When I looked at myself in the mirror, I saw the vertical line in the middle of my forehead, and deep dark shadows under my eyes caused by so much grief and lack of sleep. I thought, *I look like a freak,* so I put on a bunch of makeup and off to work I would go. It took a lot of energy to hide my inner turmoil.

After a while, I noticed that people did not study me as closely as I thought. I realized they were more focused on themselves to notice me, so it got easier to continue and excel in my "acting career." I did my job and interacted with people on a superficial level. I still wasn't getting any sleep, but I would lay there at night and my body would get just enough energy to drudge through another day.

One day, my mother informed me that a family from Canada had an accident, and many of them were at Harborview, Seattle's best trauma hospital. She asked me if I could go and help a daughter who had suffered a fractured spine and a head injury. I went with my mother to visit this family, and when I saw Daciana at the hospital, her hair was matted up in a big glob of dried blood. Her head had been scalped, starting just above her hairline as she flew through the windshield of the van. The doctors had pulled the skin back together and stitched it.

Daciana was in and out of sleep, but she was worried about her hair most of all because she was engaged to be married. I told her I would come back later in the afternoon after her treatments and tests and try to work on detangling her hair. I came back in the afternoon and I worked for a long time cleaning her hair with mineral oils and soap. As I worked on her hair, I kept thinking, *Why am I trying to save her vanity? She doesn't even realize that she has the most important thing still within her. She has life, and she can feel the love of those around her.* From the doctor's reports, I knew that her spine would heal in a couple of months with the help of a body brace, and her head injury was not severe enough that it would cause permanent brain damage.

Some of the nurses there asked me who I was and what my profession was since I knew so much about Daciana's medical condition. When they heard I was a nurse, they said I should apply for a job there because Harborview was hiring. I decided maybe I should try it. I applied, got the job, and started working in their acute care unit. We were working with AIDS patients, drug addicts, alcoholics, and trauma patients. It was interesting to work with them, and I could relate to them in many ways. Many of the patients had no hope, just like me, yet I was now able to function and act in a decent, socialized way. I provided the best care I could and did quite well as a nurse and "actor." Somehow the fast pace took me away from my thoughts because I had to focus on the job, so I found some temporary relief.

7

GETTING MARRIED

One day in October of 1996, my sister Natalia and I were driving to Northgate to pick up my paycheck from the nursing agency. As I was driving, my sister noticed a familiar street where she had recently been to a bridal shower, and asked if I would mind if we stopped by the house so she could say hi to her friend.

She thought I might like to meet Ion while she would visit with her friend, George. She told me that Ion, the house owner, was a charming man about my age. She told me that he had gone to a Christian college, was volunteering at the Romanian church and was translating some of the sermons. I said, "Sure, whatever."

We were met outside by the car by an acquaintance who was visiting Ion at the time, also. After a bit of small talk, we went inside, and he introduced me to Ion as my sister mingled with her friend, George. Ion was playing

Chess with another friend. His dining table was attractively set for four with a black tablecloth, and blue and orange ceramic plates coordinated with silverware that had matching blue handles. The house was attractive, and the friends were welcoming. I said I loved to play Chess, and Ion said we should play sometime.

I met Ion again after Romanian church a couple of days later. At that time, I started to attend a small American church in Lynwood where I was invited by a missionary couple I had known before, and who had been praying for me as they knew about my recent struggles. That little church had a tradition of going to lunch together at a restaurant after the morning service; that one particular day I ended up sitting next to Darren, the kid who played the keyboard. He was a young, black man who was delighted to meet me, and as he did not have a ride home, I offered to drive him.

On the way, I said something about the Romanian church I had gone to before and that I was probably going to attend there that evening with my parents. Darren said he would love to visit the Romanian church as he had never been to any church where they spoke a different language, so I ended up taking him by our house where he met my family, and then we went to the Romanian church together that evening.

After church, Ion had invited a bunch of young people to a restaurant to hang out, and he invited me and Darren, too. Later that week, Ion called me and invited me to go bowling with him. He said he was concerned about me dating Darren because he knew some girls who had dated "that type of guy" and ended up getting hurt. Ion lived in the ghettos in Chicago as a teenager, and he said something about how Darren reminded him of the troublesome kids in that neighborhood. Ion and I never went bowling that night since it snowed, and all the bowling places were closed. We ended up at a fancy Red Robin in downtown Bellevue.

Ion was a straightforward guy. He shared some pretty crazy stories about his army days and I thought, maybe he was just as crazy as I am. Ion listened to me as I talked about the way I felt and what had happened to me recently. He encouraged me and said that he didn't think there was no hope for me. He kept saying that the grace of God is enough. Ion would say, "Have you trusted Christ to save you and take you to heaven?" And I would say, "Of course, I accepted Christ when I was younger and prayed the sinner's prayer, but I'm not sure His grace applies to me anymore since I feel God has removed Himself from me, and everything that has to do with life was removed from my heart." But Ion just kept saying that these feelings are temporary and that I should stop paying so much attention to them.

Ion accepted me as I was. He spent time with me and drove me to work in the snow with his 4-wheeler for the next few weeks. I should mention, too, that my perception of time and space were also altered after the breakdown. I would drive fast and not feel the speed; in fact, it would feel slow to me. My perception of danger was altered. One time, when Ion was driving me to work on an icy winter morning, he hit a patch of ice and started to slide, and I laughed and told him to stop playing at the wheel. I thought he was swerving like that on purpose.

Well, Ion was very nice. He said he loved me, and he did everything he could to encourage me. After a short period of dating, he asked me to marry him. I would lay my head on his chest sometimes when he sang and listen to his heartbeat, hoping that the song in his heart would somehow transfer to me. I accepted his marriage proposal since he accepted me and said he loved me the way I was. I had shared my fears that I wasn't sure I would be able to be the wife of his dreams, but he reassured me that things would work out fine.

My dad was not so sure I should marry him and would say, "Are you sure you want to marry this guy? He doesn't seem like your type, he wasn't exactly respectful at dinner the other night." In spite of my dad's comments, I said to myself, *If no one stops me or tells me not to marry Ion, then I will marry him. But if someone says I shouldn't marry him, I will consider waiting for a better option.* No one said I shouldn't marry him, they would just say, "Are you sure about that?"

When people ask my husband, Ion, how we met, he says, "She just showed up at my doorstep one day. I was just thinking about getting serious with a girl I had been dating when a thought came to my mind as though God was saying, 'What about God's will for your life?'"

Ion shares about how two or three years back he saw me in the Romanian church parking lot when he first visited there, and it was like he heard someone say to him, "That girl is God's will for your life." Then his good friend, Tudor, who noticed Ion was looking in my direction, said to him at the same time, "I think that girl is God's will for your life." He didn't get to meet me that day. Apparently, I got into my dad's car and we drove off before Ion could introduce himself. Anyway, as Ion was playing Chess with his friend and thinking about the girl he was dating, the thought of, "What about God's will for your life?" played in his mind. *Well, if she shows up at my door in the next 10 seconds I will reconsider.* And that's when I knocked on his door.

We were married three months later, and things seemed alright for a while. We'd meet with friends, go to movies, and go out to eat often. I cooked and cleaned, and worked at Harborview 3-4 days a week. Ion ran his construction business during the day, and his janitorial business at night.

We took some long vacations and spent some time at different resorts and did everything we could to enjoy life together, but, somehow, we could not really connect, and our relationship grew colder and colder. Neither of us really opened up to talk about how we felt. There seemed to be a thick wall between us that was making communication impossible. It seemed that no matter how hard I tried to be a good wife to Ion, he enjoyed my company less and less. Ion did not care to go to church on Sundays, and it didn't seem important to him to connect emotionally.

Ion encouraged me to start a consulting business for adult family homes and I became very successful at that, but no matter what I did, whether I worked at the hospital or went on vacation or worked with my business, I was dissatisfied. We had been married now for almost three years and we had no children. I told Ion even before we got married that I didn't think I could have any children due to the stuff I went through. Ion reassured me at that time that it would be alright with him if we had no children of our own. "We can always adopt some," he said, "if you can't have any kids, so don't worry."

$\int$

A RAY OF HOPE

Although Ion and I attended church while we dated, Ion decided not to go to church anymore after we got married. I felt embarrassed to go to the church where people knew us without him, so I didn't go, either. The pastor from the Lynwood church called me to see how things were going. I just told him that Ion had decided not to go to his church anymore for some reason, but I didn't tell him that we were not going to church anywhere.

After a while, I thought I would try going to church again without Ion, and see if I could get some answers for the way I still felt inside. I went to different churches every week since it seemed I could not connect with God or anyone. I still felt a bubble around me, and nothing could penetrate. I tried reading the Bible and praying, but I couldn't read more than a few passages; like church and everything else, reading the Bible was not encouraging to me. And as for praying, it felt like I was talking to the wall.

One day, I got tired of trying and not getting anywhere and I thought to myself, *I will try one more time with God and if He doesn't do something I will quit trying and continue 'acting' and doing the best I can with my wretched existence.*

That Sunday morning, I took a piece of paper, folded it, and tore it in four pieces. On three of the pieces, I wrote the names of three different churches. One of them was a big non-denominational church in the area that I attended sometimes. Another was the Romanian church my parents were attending, and the third one I found in the phone book, under Assemblies of God churches. I figured they are usually pretty correct doctrinally from everything that I had learned so far, and the name of the pastor rang a bell to me; I thought maybe I heard him on the radio before. The fourth piece of paper I left blank, and I said to myself, *If I draw the blank one, that will mean that God really doesn't care about me, not now and not ever, so why keep trying.* But I told God in my silent prayer that I would try the church that comes up in the lots for a while. I would give Him a good chance to show me that He cares for me. I didn't pray out loud, because I thought to myself, *The devil can hear and get in the middle of it, but God would know my thoughts.*

So, I cast the lots and drew the piece of paper. My grandfather used to cast lots like that sometimes when he had to make a decision. That's why I thought I would cast lots. So, I drew the piece of paper. It was the new church. I called for the directions and got an answering machine explaining the time of the services and how to get there, so I went to the 10:00 am service. I sat in the last row of seats. Pastor Randy, one of the worship leaders, was leading the whole service that day. He had long, curly hair, and looked like a rebel in my mind.

The way I was raised, guys with long hair like that were considered rebels, and the kind of music he played would also be considered rebellious. He introduced a song he had composed called, "The Nine-Mile Dancing." He said that King David, when he brought back the Ark of the Covenant from captivity, was so filled with joy that he danced in an abandoned fashion before God and all the people. Pastor Randy explained that some Bible scholars estimated the distance of that joyous procession to have been about nine miles long. Everyone in the church sang and danced as they worshiped, and they looked like they had real joy. They really looked like they were experiencing God's presence.

The whole church just seemed filled with this incredible presence of God. Throughout the worship service I sobbed uncontrollably, not because I felt God's presence or any joy, but because the pain of my emptiness and deadness intensified. I wanted so much to have that kind of freedom and joy, but there was none. There wasn't even a glimmer of hope I could hold on to.

A man greeted me at the end of the service and introduced himself as Dr. Mike. Although I had not talked about my problems freely with anyone outside of my family for a long time, I felt safe explaining how I felt to Dr. Mike. He prayed for me and encouraged me to come back. During the offering, I put my name and phone number on a card with a comment that I wanted prayer.

In the weeks that followed, a woman named Christine called me once or twice a week and asked me if she could pray for me. I would say, "Yes," and I would listen to her prayers. She would always ask me if there was something specific I needed prayer for and I would always say, "I still feel hopeless and dead inside." But her prayers somehow encouraged me to continue attending the weekly Sunday service.

After about 6 weeks, I was introduced to a home group where people from church met during the week to talk, pray, and get to know each other. The first time I attended, there were only three men, one woman, and myself. The other people that normally attended the home group were gone to help at a mission. After a few worship songs, we sat down, and everyone shared about what God was doing in their life that week. They all shared concrete and beautiful answers to prayers and were so excited about how God was with them and leading them in such an amazing way.

When they were all done sharing, the group leader asked, "So, what about you?" I said, "Well, it's great that you can all say that God is doing something in your lives, but I am completely hopeless." I broke down and cried and shared how dead I felt inside; how I felt that God and everything pertaining to life was drained out of me.

The group leader said with a warm smile, "Sounds like you gotta get in 'the chair.'" Bob set a chair in the middle of the room, and the group gathered around me to pray. Bob asked, "Did you receive Christ as your Lord and Savior? You know, the Bible says that if you believe in Jesus with your heart, and you confess Him with your mouth you will be saved."

I said, "I know that in theory I have confessed before, but I feel like it was all nullified at the time of my breakdown, and I feel there is no hope for me." I said that I felt God rejected me because I had committed the unpardonable sin; I had sinned willfully after having received grace.

"Well," Bob continued, "all it says here is that if you confess your sin, He is faithful and just to forgive you and cleanse you from all unrighteousness. It does not say that you will feel forgiven, but you have to take it by faith. That faith is not seeing or feeling, but a commitment to take God at His Word and wait for Him to work out the details."

Bob asked, "Would you like to recommit your life to God, then?"

"Of course!" I replied.

"Ok, pray after me" he said, and proceeded to pray something like, "Jesus, I believe that You died for all my sins, and I confess all my sins and ask for Your forgiveness; and I confess You as my Lord from now on. Amen." I repeated after him, even though it seemed like I was just going through the motions. I really wanted God and I wanted Him to know I meant business. I wanted to do whatever it took. After this, I thought maybe there was a little tiny ray of hope even though I still felt as dead. I said, "Well maybe this is a start."

The group members took turns praying for me, and Bob encouraged me to continue to come to the home-group, and continue to tell myself even if I didn't feel anything that I was saved because of the promise of God. Every time I would go to the home-group, they would pray for me and encourage me to keep trusting God no matter how I felt. They really cared about me. No one judged me, no one cared about my past mistakes or failures, and no one ever asked what sin I had committed. They just continued to tell me to look ahead and keep trusting Jesus.

I was invited to many small parties that were going on at one church member's house or another in the weeks and months to come, and it was nice to have my time occupied getting together with people who seemed to really care about me. I met new people at these parties and at the church meetings.

Frequently, someone would speak to me as if they knew exactly what I was thinking. I remember one time the question came to my mind, *Does God even care about how I feel?*, and a few seconds later a woman came behind me and said, "God knows exactly how you feel, and He wants you to know He cares." Many times, people would ask to pray for me during the worship service or after the service and would mention in their prayers specific issues I was struggling with that they had no way of knowing about. Some of the women in the church befriended me and took me to lunch or came to visit me at home.

My husband was mostly gone during this time, either working or visiting casinos, though he made me believe for the longest time that he was just running the janitorial business at night. He didn't mind it if I was going to church or some church function. I asked him many times if he would come with me, but he was either not interested or too tired.

On Sundays, Pastor Mark's teachings were very relevant and seemed to always speak directly to me and to some issue I was struggling with. And the worship services: I think I cried straight through each one of them the first few months because I wanted to have a song in my heart again, but even the beat of the drum seemed to echo in my chest as it would in an empty room. I cried and wished that I could have the freedom to even raise my hands or lift my eyes off the ground. I wished I could dance for joy like they were.

When I was growing into my early twenties, before the whole breakdown, I thought it was unnecessary to shout to God, and I was taught dancing in the church was just not done. In fact, dancing of any kind was considered sensual and sinful. I thought, *God is a God of order and a church service should be orderly and quiet.* But now I decided that if God would give back my heart, He deserved my praises in all abandonment of self, not thinking about what anyone else thought about me.

It is significant to mention some things here about my grandfather, who was a devoted man of God. He was raised in a Baptist church and attended the Baptist School of Theology in Bucharest. He was ordained as a pastor and worked in the local church in his little village for many years. As he was doing some mission work among the gypsies that lived in the surrounding areas, he experienced the baptism of the Holy Spirit through speaking in tongues. It wasn't that he was studying the subject of speaking in tongues or pursuing God to give him that gift; it just happened to him in one of the meetings while on that mission trip. He went on to practice this gift in his private prayer life.

My grandfather continued to pastor the Baptist church for a while, but since he practiced speaking in tongues in his personal prayer time, the church leadership excommunicated him, stating that he had "pentecostal deviation."

Papó went on to open his home for all who would come, and started a little church there. He was ordained by the leaders of the Pentecostal church as an overseer for many churches in the region. He was a great preacher and teacher. I always enjoyed listening to him as I grew up. He was very dynamic, and I would never get bored when he was at the pulpit. He had a way of bringing a Bible story to life like no one else.

Andras Bacsi, who the village people called Papó, was basically the one man in the village that everybody brought their broken things to and he would fix them. They would pay him either in money or other goods, whatever they could give. He would fix their pots and pans, their stoves, their door locks, you name it. When we came to visit, we would knock on his door and say, "Készen van a fazakam? (is my pot ready?)" That was the one phrase that we heard when people came to pick up their patched pots.

Everyone knew him as the man of God, and he would always listen to people and have a good and encouraging word for anyone that needed it. My older brother, my younger sister, and I would spend just about every school break at his house in the village of Samsom.

It was a cute little house that Papó and Grandma had built themselves out of mud bricks. There was no gas or electricity at that time. They used a little oil lamp for light at night, and a wood stove for cooking and heating. The house was actually not so little if you counted the addition that was built toward the street side of the house, but that addition was used as Grampa's workshop and storage, and never got finished. The main house consisted of two rooms upstairs and two basement rooms.

Those are the best childhood memories. We would eat breakfast on the front porch where we would do our gymnastics, too, climbing on the railing and hanging from the top wooden bar. We would eat freshly picked raspberries, fresh cucumbers, feta cheese from the village farm, and fresh eggs that grandma's chicken laid.

The view from the porch was magnificent. There was a row of poplar trees behind a few gardens that were next to the village school. Behind those trees were many hills where people had their vineyards. We would go from time to time to tend to Papó's vineyard or we would look for mushrooms in the woods behind the vineyard. Sometimes we would sit by the pond next to the woods and weave frog-catcher baskets out of tall grasses.

Papó and Irenka Mama always had us involved with the household chores. We picked veggies and flowers from the garden, and fruits and nuts from the trees, sorted beans, and plucked the chickens after Papó would chop off their heads. On Sundays, we would wake up and help turn the main room into the church sanctuary by rearranging the furniture and decorating. The wood stove was on the left as you entered the room, and on the right there were two beds, one next to another. Towards the back of the room, there was a large square table with a long storage bench behind it. We would set up extra benches and chairs next to the beds and around the table.

For church, Grampa sat on one corner of the bench and used the table corner as the pulpit. The kids would sit mostly on the benches around the table, with the adults sitting behind them on the edges of the beds and on the benches. We would prepare songs during the week and would take turns writing the new songs we learned in the gigantic songbook that was like the centerpiece of the table. Next to the big songbook sat the oil lamp that was used only in the evenings. On the right side of the room, past the stove and next to the window, was an interesting piece of furniture; a kind of storage dresser with a straw mattress in it which was used for a bed at night and a sliding table top to cover it during the day.

In 1990, when my parents went to Romania to visit, they arranged for Grandpa to come to the United States to live with us as he was recovering from illness and was very weak. He recovered, and went back the next year to be with grandma. Then in 1992, Dad was able to arrange for both of them to come live in the States.

One morning in May of 1999, Papó and Grandma Irenka were doing their morning Bible reading and prayer, as usual. They often sang together, and that morning grandpa sang a song that is sung at funerals back in their village in Romania. The song was about getting a crown in heaven after finishing well on earth.

Grandma said she was surprised at how well he sang. His voice had been weak and scratchy in recent months, but on that day his voice was strong and clear. She joined in the singing and when the song ended, Papó started to pray. He gave thanks and prayed for their children. He lay down to rest and asked grandma to continue praying for the grandchildren.

As grandma was praying for us, Grandpa fell asleep. Around lunchtime, Dad called him to come to the dining room table for lunch. He did not respond, and Dad went into their bedroom to check on Grandpa. He called out, shook him and sprinkled water over his face, but he did not wake up. He checked his blood pressure, pulse, and blood glucose. Everything was normal. His breathing was fine, too.

When mom came home from work a couple of hours later and checked his eyes by pulling his eyelids back, she saw that his pupils were fixed, and his body was completely paralyzed. After talking with the doctor, mother announced for everyone to come and say good-bye. She knew it wouldn't be long until he would die. He looked so peaceful, as though he was taking a nap. The next morning, shortly after Grandma finally got the courage to come near him and say goodbye, he took his final breath.

Papó lifted his hands and crossed them on his chest. Then he lifted his head as though he wanted to go up, and exhaled for the last time. It was as though he had asked God to be able to move his body one last time to show Grandma and my mom that he was at peace and ready to go, and God granted his request.

Papó died a beautiful death on the day of Pentecost, when the church celebrates the first outpouring of the Holy Spirit.

The day we buried him, there was a very interesting

yet comforting phenomenon in the sky. The clouds had formed a circle around the sun on a very large perimeter, and there was a beautiful silver lining around that umbrella of clouds. He was buried here in Seattle, but the same phenomenon happened back in his village when they rang the church bells to commemorate him the next day. The village people were heard saying, "It's the glory of God receiving András Bácsi into eternity."

To me, it was significant that Grandpa died on the day of Pentecost, which is the day we celebrate the first manifestation of the Holy Spirit being released on the believers of the early church after the death and resurrection of Christ. It was like God was validating Grandpa and celebrating him by receiving him into eternity, even though many people in his village had rejected him or ridiculed him because he believed differently and had practiced the gift of speaking in tongues like the first believers had experienced.

As for myself, even though I was raised in a church that believed in the gifts of the Holy Spirit including the speaking in tongues, I was still drawn to a Baptist church and spent a lot of time there because I did not like the prayers in my church where everyone prayed loudly and all at the same time. It just seemed so disorderly.

As I listened to Pastor Mark, I recognized how I had misunderstood so much. He taught about our responsibility to worship Jesus and acknowledge Him, and to trust that He would fight the battle for us. He taught about the way God's logic is above ours and how sometimes His way seems upside down to us or opposite of what we would normally think. I started to raise my hands during worship ever so timidly and started to sing louder. I just sang out of my throat because I didn't have a heart from which to sing. At least that is how I continued to feel.

Pastor Mark talked about how Christ came, "to bind up the brokenhearted,… to proclaim the acceptable year of the Lord" (Isaiah 61:1-2 KJV). I would read on in my Bible: "To appoint unto them that mourn in Zion, to give unto them beauty for ashes, the oil of joy for mourning, the garment of praise for the spirit of heaviness; that they might be called trees of righteousness, the planting of the LORD, that he might be glorified. And they shall build the old wastes, they shall raise up the former desolations, and they shall repair the waste cities" (Isaiah 61:3-4 KJV).

I felt desolated and like a waste, but I said to myself, *I will hold on to these Bible verses and hope that God will repair me because He is the only one that could do it if He wanted to.* I thought that maybe somehow God's mercy would override His justice in the end.

9

THUNDER AND LIGHTNING

In January of the year 2000, the church had a Sunday set aside to pray for women who were unable to conceive. I had no children, and according to the tests I had done up to that time, I was not even ovulating. I decided to go up to the front and ask God to allow me to have at least one child at some point in my life. A couple from church prayed for me, and that was that. I forgot all about it. I didn't want to think about having children at that time because I did not want to be disappointed.

Sometime in June, Ion had to go to the emergency room to see a doctor because he was feeling really nauseated after eating out at a restaurant that day. I went with him, and as we were waiting for the doctor, I noticed I was feeling queasy a little bit, too. A couple of days later, I went with Ion to our family doctor for a follow-up. I mentioned that I had felt nauseated, also, when Ion was in the ER the other day, even though I did not eat at that restaurant. The doctor decided to do a couple of tests for me as well. A few days later the doctor called me at work, and to my surprise, he informed me that I was pregnant.

I did not have any of the usual signs of pregnancy up until then; if I did, I did not notice. I was in the process of changing jobs, and I did not tell my new supervisor and co-workers that I was pregnant. Somehow, I wanted to deny it still. On my orientation day I fainted during training. I went to the emergency room to see what was wrong. My supervisor thought that maybe I had a seizure. I still didn't say anything. She said, "Maybe you're pregnant." "I guess it's possible," I responded. Sure enough, the urine test came back positive. That was my grand entrance to Evergreen Hospital where I was training to work in the critical care unit.

A few days later, I had some bleeding and I thought, *There goes my pregnancy*. I was referred to an OB doctor right away who did an ultrasound, right there in his office. I was even more surprised to learn that the baby was already about 14 weeks. The ultrasound showed that the baby was well, but there was an area on my uterus that was bleeding. The doctor said, "Go home and take it easy for a while."

The next week I was bleeding again at work, so I told my supervisor and got sent to see my OB doctor. That day, my home group leader's mother was my patient in our unit. I went to tell her that another nurse had to take my place. I told her and her daughters that I had to go see my doctor because maybe I was going to lose the baby. The daughters started to pray right there, asking God to heal me and save the baby.

I had another ultrasound that afternoon and I was still bleeding from the same spot on my uterus, but the baby was fine. I got put on bedrest for a week. My home group friends helped make the week of resting in bed much easier. They called me to encourage me and pray for me. Some came and brought me food, and some brought books to read. Someone came almost every day that week, and they prayed for me at their home group meeting. After that week the bleeding stopped, and my pregnancy continued in a normal fashion.

In January, as I was preparing for labor, Pastor Mark

asked me if I could give a testimony on "Conception Sunday" since I got prayed for last January. I said I would if I didn't go into labor by then, but on Saturday my labor started, and I left a message that I would not be coming to give my testimony because the baby was coming. Sunday morning Pastor Mark announced, "Well I have bad news and good news today; the bad news is that the lady who was to give testimony is not here, but the good news is that she's at the hospital in labor, so let's all pray for her to have a safe delivery!" Someone told me later that the whole church stood up prayed that my labor would go well.

At the hospital, the delivery nurse was so helpful. She knew exactly which muscle I should relax, and had the most fitting words to help me work through each contraction. She would tell Ion what he could do to help me relax, and amazingly her methods were very effective. Caroline, a friend from church, offered to be there with me as I was going through labor as well. Her presence and prayers were so helpful. That evening, our little Wolfgang was born without any problems, and the labor and delivery process was definitely blessed.

I had decided during my pre-labor visits that I would try natural labor for as long as possible. Part of the motivation for me was that although I had accepted with my mind that I was forgiven, I was still living with the fear that God's judgment could still result in hell for me. In my mind the conversation would go like: *If God still decides to send me to hell when I die, I should try to see how much pain I can endure and see if there is any way I could brace myself for it.*

There was a real war going on in my head. On one hand, I put my trust in God, but on the other hand, I listened to the old thoughts of defeat and failure. Still, God gave me the grace minute by minute, and I saw at the end how His provision was there all along.

The way little Wolfgang was born a year to the date from the time of the prayer was a real sign to me that God really did care about me. Our baby was so beautiful, and he brought me a certain kind of joy. Still, the feelings of deadness in my heart continued.

The church was so supportive of our little family before and after Wolfgang was born. They prayed for my pregnancy to go well. They put on a baby shower for me and prayed for everything to go well with my pregnancy and labor, and God did answer those prayers in such an amazing way.

Ion and I talked about whether we wanted more kids or not and looked into the idea of using contraceptives, but it just didn't seem right. We came to the conclusion that since God gave us our firstborn in such a miraculous way, He knew best how many kids we should have. We said, "If He opened the womb, He will close it when He sees fit."

God gave us our second son, Anthony, a year and a half later. My husband was not able to be there when I went into labor with him, but my mother came with me to the hospital while my dad watched little Wolfgang. When I saw how much it helped me having Caroline there when Wolfgang was born, I asked Janet, a lady from the home-group I attended, if she would come and be with me through my labor and delivery. The home group had become so much like a real family to me and I had come to depend upon them. I craved their encouragement and support.

Not having my husband there was very hard, and at one point, I didn't want to keep working through those really intense contractions, so I pleaded for the epidural. It seemed to take forever for the doctor on call to come and set it up. When he finally came and got the tray and the team ready, Anthony was ready and was born within a couple of minutes. I was so thankful the epidural was not needed after all.

Wolfgang had just started walking, and now we had baby Anthony, a jolly little brother. Somehow, I had just enough energy to take care of him, too. We had hired a live-in nanny so I could continue to work at the hospital and expand my home business as well. There was never a dull moment.

We nicknamed the two boys "thunder and lightning," and sometimes the nanny called Wolfgang "the little type-writer," because his steps sounded like an old typewriter when he would get up in the mornings and run around. He started walking before he turned eight months old. Actually, he didn't walk much. He mostly ran. He would fall often, but he would get right back up and keep going. He was fearless and quick. Anthony, on the other hand, she nicknamed, "the dinosaur." His steps were heavy and stompy. It seemed like God provided just in time for everything and a little more joy was added to my life, but I still struggled and still felt very much incomplete and insecure in my identity and standing with God.

10

BREAKTHROUGH

In April 2004, there was a women's conference at our church and I decided to go. I had to make special arrangements because I had just started a training course for caregivers, and had a class scheduled at the same time as part of the conference.

At the beginning of the conference, a young couple was performing a dance. The young man was a picture of God the Father and the young lady signified a woman, any woman.

> "You raise me up, so I can stand on mountains.
> You raise me up, to walk on stormy seas.
> I am strong when I am on your shoulders.
> You raise me up...to more than I can be."[1]

The song played as a young man lifted the girl on his

shoulder. It was a beautiful picture of how the Father in Heaven wants a relationship like that with His daughters on earth. That whole dance had quite an impact on me. I cried through the song, wishing that I could have that kind of relationship with God, where I would feel loved and safe in His arms. At the end of the conference there was a time of worship and prayer. I started to get more and more into the worship during the Sunday services, and by this time I had resolved that I would praise God 'til I died no matter how I felt just because He deserves to be worshiped, and that I would trust that somehow He would work things out. In fact, I said to myself that even if He decides to send me to hell, I was still going to worship Him until my last breath and keep appealing to Him in hopes that His mercy would somehow be stronger in the end.

So, at the conference, I lifted my hands and sang as loud as I could. While we were worshiping I had the impression that I was holding a little lamb in my right hand, lifting him up for God to see. The Lamb, of course, signified Jesus, and I was showing that He took my place. At the end of the conference, the speaker encouraged us to come up for prayer. During the prayer, I told God in desperation that I wanted to feel His love in my heart, that I couldn't live anymore with this total deadness in my chest, and that I really wanted to feel like a daughter rather than a stranger to God.

After a few minutes of desperately crying out to God, I felt an infusion in my chest, like God came back and life came back. I felt like God became my Father, my Daddy, and He was holding me close to His heart and telling me how much He loves me. I laughed and cried, "Daddy, I love you. Daddy, I love you." I thanked Him for restoring me and making me a whole person again. Shelly, the wife of my home group leader, was behind me during the prayer, and I turned and embraced her and cried for joy on her shoulder for the longest time. I felt that my heart was restored and there was nothing to fear anymore.

That week I was full of joy. I felt like I was flying. I was so full that I couldn't even eat much. I slept deeply at night and felt incredibly refreshed. I would wake up after four or five hours to pray and thank God, and pray for everybody that came to my mind. I told Ion what had happened, and how I felt that God had finally restored my heart and my life. I think he was kind of shocked. He just looked at me and didn't say anything. I think he wanted to see the long-term effects first. I called my dad to tell him what happened, and I went to see him. My mom was excited, too, and she said, "I knew that God would help you understand that He really cares for you, but I didn't know when and how He would go about helping you see that." I gave my dad a great big hug; I cried on his shoulder and he cried for joy.

I called Tim Emerson, a guest pastor I met at church who had a ministry for women. God used him over the past four years to help me understand some of the reasons why these things happened to me. I was so excited. I told many people at work. I told the people in my church home group, too. I just couldn't shut up about it. I was feeling really alive! I would look at the squirrels in our backyard and would cry for joy. They were running up the tree and would stop to look at me as if they were acknowledging my joy as well. Nature came alive again also; I could once again enjoy its beauty and it didn't feel like still life anymore. I emailed my friends on the net. I would get up and get my office work done speedily, and then I would spend time with the kids and enjoy them, as I felt I could now give them real love.

It was like I was on cloud nine that whole year. I shared with everyone about my experiences with God, and I was so excited. One day, I shared with a social worker at work and she cautioned me that I might want to be careful how I talked about some of my experiences, as things could be interpreted differently and could affect my career. I thought that was wise advice, and I was more careful about what I shared and with whom, especially at work.

Being pregnant with our third son, Conrad, was like a walk in the park. He must have been conceived right after that conference in April. I didn't make a big deal about being pregnant. I was at peace with having more kids, and the pregnancy was easy. I enjoyed doing my Denise Austin pregnancy workout videos to stay in shape.

When it was time for Conrad to be born, about four days after my due date, I was literally trying jumping jacks to get labor started. I had done my 20-minute video exercises just about every day that week, and on that February morning I started to have light contractions just about five minutes apart. I took a relaxing bath and the contractions kept up consistently, so I decided it was time to go in, even though the contractions weren't intense at all.

When we got to the hospital, the intake nurse said, "Let's put her in the triage room, she doesn't look like she's really in labor." I had called my good doula and friend, Diana, who was my pick for a helper this time, and she came within the hour.

My OB doctor showed up to check me around that time, also, and said enthusiastically, "Let's have this baby!" She asked me a couple of questions about my preferences, and decided it would be a good idea to break my water. She did, and a couple of contractions later I was ready to push, and Conrad was born. It was like I never had any pain with his birth. Such grace was provided. I was really amazed. Conrad was born at about 7:30 that morning and by 7 p.m. I was home. Normally, women were kept overnight after birthing in the hospital, but the doctor said she would discharge me early, considering I was a nurse and knew what to do.

Next came Lance, a couple of years later. It seemed we had a baby every other year. One of the cardiologists that checked on the patients on our floor asked sarcastically one day, "Are you perpetually pregnant?" "Not really," I replied. To me, perpetual meant having a baby every year. I had seen a few women like that. I thought God was spacing them just right for us.

Lance came a bit early. He was the only one that broke my water naturally. The doctor decided to induce my labor because natural labor just wasn't starting fast enough. We wanted the birth to be as natural as possible, so I chose not to have the epidural.

Joyce, a woman from church who had befriended me, came to help me when it was time for labor and delivery. She was such a gift. She knew just what to say with each contraction to help me. She knew just when and how and what muscle I should relax. Ion was there, too, and we laughed and talked through the entire five hours plus of intense induced labor. "Piece of cake," we said afterward.

Sometime during labor, Joyce had shared about some things she read in a book titled, *Supernatural Childbirth* by Jackie Mize, and we all agreed we could put this labor in that category.

After Lance was born, I quit my job at the hospital so that I could be with the kids more. Being away from them for twelve hours at a time was not my idea of motherhood. The older boys were getting to be school-age, and I wanted to try homeschooling them. I had enough work consulting for Adult Family Homes, and that gave me the flexibility to schedule my work around my home life.

When our fifth son, Justin, was conceived, we started looking for other insurance options since we were no longer covered by insurance through my work at the hospital. I purchased *Supernatural Childbirth* and read through it. It made a lot of sense to me, and "supernaturally" a birthing center popped up right in our neighborhood. Of course, I popped in and asked questions. To my surprise, my new insurance covered their services, so I signed up to have the next baby there.

Another reason for looking at the birthing center option was the fact that I had not checked in with the OB doctors at the hospital until quite late in this pregnancy. It was taking a long time to find insurance, and I didn't want the extra expenses out of pocket. The doctors that were available said they were not comfortable taking me on as a patient so late in my pregnancy. They said it was too risky as I was older, and did not have the usual checks early in the pregnancy. They started talking about referring me to a high-risk pregnancy specialist. I thought that was pretty presumptuous since I felt fine, and because of my nursing background I had no reason to expect this birth would be a problem. Supernaturally, God provided because this birthing center was willing to accept me as a patient, even this late in my pregnancy.

Justin was our first baby born in water. I had dreamt he was born in the bathtub, so I decided to try a water birth at the birthing center. As I prepared for Justin's birth, I read through *Supernatural Childbirth* a few times. It explained that when Eve ate the forbidden fruit, she and all women were cursed. They would have pain in childbirth. But, when Jesus died, that curse was broken for those who accept His sacrifice and come to Him in faith.

The author went on to say that we have become conditioned to think that we will have pain during childbirth. We hear it throughout life so many times; we hear the horror stories, and we accept the concept. Thinking those thoughts create fear and worry and an expectation of pain. We tend to get what we fear. However, the Bible says we need to be renewing our mind daily, which means we need to replace old thoughts and thought patterns with thoughts that are according to God's plan of salvation and redemption.

I learned from this book how to think of contractions as just muscle soreness, like the kind one experiences when they work out, instead of "labor pains." The book had many Scripture references that I could keep in mind to replace old ideas and fears. It also talked about how the Hebrew women would use a birthing stool, which helped them assume a position that allows gravity to accelerate labor and delivery. It helped me gain a new understanding that changed my perspective and expectation and really boosted my faith.

Around the same time, I happened upon a book about the life of Madame Guyon, a French woman who lived in the 1600's and became known for practicing a way of connecting with God through prayer and meditation on the Scriptures and counseling people privately in their spiritual pursuit.[2] Her writings reminded me that when we find a quiet time and place that we can dedicate to sit with God, we can take it by faith that we are actually sitting in His presence and we are having a conversation. And since God comes to dwell in us when we give our hearts to Jesus, we can hear Him in our heart when we take the time.

I had been practicing a level of worship and quiet time before and had experienced a sense of the presence of God many times, but the way it was explained in this book seemed different and made sense to me. It was such a simple concept, and it was backed up by plenty of Scripture. I said to myself, *I sure need to practice this right now as I prepare for labor.* Encouragement from the books I mentioned and my homegroup prayers for my labor and delivery helped me resist fear and panic.

About four days after the due date, after I took care of some shopping and some bank transactions for our construction business, I started to have contractions. They got stronger and more regular within an hour. I called my parents to come and take the older boys to their house, and I called Ion to come home and take me to the birthing center. He said he was in the middle of some important work, and asked if I could call my dad to see if he could take me. I said I could walk there since it was so close, but when I called the birthing center they said they would prefer I had someone drive me, just in case, so my dad took me. Joyce arrived at the center shortly after I did, and Ion finally got there about an hour later.

The midwife broke my water as we had planned, and labor started to intensify. Joyce was so good at helping me through each contraction. She said at one point, "Don't think about all the contractions that are coming up, you have enough grace for this contraction." That was such a revelation to me, and I think I will never forget that concept of being grateful for the grace that I receive for difficult encounters and trusting God through them moment by moment. Thinking like that keeps us from getting overwhelmed.

Joyce played my worship CD in the background, and I started to have an internal dialogue with Jesus. He was so present in my heart and was waiting there, listening. I said, *Why should there be so many more contractions? Can't we just skip to pushing the baby out?* Then I said it out loud to the midwife, "Can I just push this baby out?" She said, "Well, you know what your body is doing, you can try if you want to." I got into a squatting position and, all of a sudden, I felt like pushing, so I did. Then I said, "I need to wait," and the midwife confirmed, "Yes, you need to wait for the next contraction and then push with the next one."

Then in my inner conversation, I said, *Jesus, this is the hardest part. I can't do it. Can I just be like the channel and you do this through me?* At that precise moment, Justin slipped out into the water without me having to push again. The nurse washed him a little right there in the tub before bringing him out of the water to take his first breath. He cried out loudly for a couple of seconds once he was out of the water, and snuggled peacefully on my chest for a few minutes while I delivered the placenta and Ion cut the cord. He looked so beautiful and perfect. After I transferred to the bed and had Justin placed on my chest again, I realized he was the heaviest baby I had birthed so far. He was almost ten pounds. We checked into the birthing center around four o'clock that afternoon, and we were home by 10 p.m. the same day. Justin's birth was so special and definitely supernatural.

Tate was born much the same way two years later, except Joyce was not able to come. She was planning on being there, but Tate decided he was ready just about a month early, and she was on vacation. At that time, I heard Jesus say in my heart, "This one we'll do the same way, but it will be just you and Me. You're ready."

Toby was born just about an hour from the time we checked in to the birthing center. Another big baby, nine pounds plus, born in the bathtub. I wasn't completely alone; Ion and the midwife were there, but it was like God was saying, "Don't be afraid, you've got this." It was another one of those conversations I was having, with Jesus talking me through labor. Each birthing experience for me was another step of growth in my faith and understanding of who God is and how faithfully and lovingly He cared for me and provided for every little detail.

We were having boys, and we loved it. On occasion, our oldest son, Wolfgang, said he wanted a baby sister. I always looked at some girl names with each pregnancy. I had seen the name, Zayna, as I was flipping through a baby names book when I was pregnant with Conrad or Lance. I fell in love with that name and decided right then that if we ever had a girl, her name would be Zayna. Zayna means, "God is gracious" in Greek. I love that name!

One day, just out of the blue, I blurted out, "Lord, if you want me to get pregnant again and go through all that pregnancy stuff, let it be a girl this time." It wasn't like a premeditated prayer. It just came out of my mouth and then I forgot all about it.

When we found out I was pregnant about three months later, I never even thought it was going to be a girl. I was actually thinking, "It would be so cool to have seven sons."

The day before the appointment for the ultrasound, Ion said, "Oh, I'm sure it's another boy." Then, Wolfgang, our oldest son who happened to be sitting with us at the dining room table, burst into tears saying, "How could you say that? There's no way you could know that for sure." Wolfgang realized he'd touched a cord, and apologized for his insensitive remark.

The next day, the ultrasound showed we were having a girl. What a wonderful surprise that was, especially for her oldest brother, who had wanted a baby sister for so long! Then, about 24 hours later, I suddenly remembered how I had prayed to have a girl and I said to myself, *God sure has a sense of humor. He waited for me to ask specifically by gender before he gave me a girl.*

Zayna is the icing on the cake. She is such a wonderful addition to our family. When I started going into labor with her, I experienced an overwhelming feeling like something was going wrong, and I was starting to panic. I called my midwife, and she explained that my body was just letting me know it was resetting to go into labor mode. She asked me what I would normally do to relax. When Tate was almost two years old, I had been introduced to the benefits of essential oils by my good friend, Sonia, and had used some of them to help Tate relax and go to sleep.

The word "relax" reminded me of the essential oils, and that I had also studied a little about using oils in childbirth, so I said, "Maybe I could try my essential oils." The midwife had experience with them as well, and she asked me which ones I had at the house. I had some lavender oil and some "Peace and Calming." So I used each one, alternating them every few minutes. The oils were very effective, and I ended up using them throughout labor and delivery. I also looked up some Scriptures and was really inspired and encouraged.

A few hours later, Ion drove me to the birthing center. I had back labor with Zayna like I did with Wolfgang. With back labor, the baby's head pushes against the mother's spine, making labor a little trickier. Joyce had just the right ideas to ease those intense contractions. I was so glad she was able to be there this time.

My "twin" sister, Natalia, was also planning to come. She got on the road as soon as she got the message that I was at the birthing center. She's not really my twin, but we get along so well, and we look more alike since we're the two brunettes in the family. I wondered why this delivery was taking longer, and started to argue with Jesus a little bit in my inner conversation. Natalia arrived just as Zayna was born. She had to be there for some reason to see her birth.

11

LIFE AS AN ADVENTURE

I think of life as an adventure now. I thank God for allowing me to go through all that pain in the last 20 or so years, because I would have never really known Him otherwise. I would have continued to be an ignorant "good little Christian," living my life and trying to help others without real understanding, without real answers, without true joy, and without really being able to empathize with people.

Now, when I tell my story, it's like I'm giving out fresh water. It brings hope to people who are suffering, and many people tell me they are encouraged when I share bits and pieces as the occasion arises. I love to hear other people's stories and adventures with God, too.

Every day is an adventure. I'm grateful every morning for one more day of grace, and though there's a lot to do, I look forward to it instead of dreading it. Some days are harder, some are easier and feel lighter. Some days I feel exhausted and other days I feel energized, but there is an expectancy and a hope that wasn't there before.

I find that the more time I spend getting to know God, the better my day goes. The more I seek to know God through reading the Bible, praying, reading commentaries and books, listening for what God is saying to me through the Sunday morning sermons in church, watching sermons or teachings online, talking to others in small group settings, and listening to or reading testimonies, the more I learn about God. As I experience Him, the more amazed I am.

Every day is an amazing adventure of discovering one aspect or another of God's amazing love, wisdom, and power. I draw on Him to be my source and to help me through everyday life. I draw on God to help me with the mundane things I'm not so fond of, like cleaning house and closets and doing the laundry. I find joy even in those things. I don't always do a great job at it, and that's okay. Sometimes I hire help so I can focus on other priorities related to my husband or our children. I trust God to help me figure out priorities, plan my day, and delegate chores. I'm always amazed at the way God provides the energy and understanding I need to get things done.

Then there is the adventure of trusting God for my marriage. Our marriage has gone through some real ups and downs. Some breakdowns have been very traumatic, and it's amazing we're still together today. A couple of times I didn't know how to handle the intense tensions, and in my desperation, I packed up the kids and stayed with my parents until we worked things out.

I'm not proud of my decision to separate during those times, and if I knew then what I know now, I may not have separated. I'm grateful for those times now as I can relate to so many who are hurting in their marriages, and I can encourage them. Ion and I don't see many things the same way and we've had to make many adjustments, but we both decided to commit to God, to stick to our marriage vows, and see each day as a new day with new possibilities for goodness and grace. We've learned to accept each other as God's gift.

I've learned to focus more on Ion's good qualities, and be more understanding when my expectations aren't met.

We've learned to be quick to forgive and to ask for forgiveness. I've learned to focus on changing me instead of expecting Ion to change the things I would have him change. Someday I hope we will co-write a book about the subject of our marriage, but for now it's fun to just enjoy the daily adventure of it.

Then there is the adventure of raising our children and helping them grow in character and develop the self-discipline that will help them succeed. Each one of them is so unique and wonderful. Each one of them knows how to push our buttons, too, and we keep working on learning how to respond with love and patience while helping them understand and embrace the boundaries we set for their own protection.

The process of learning to trust God with our children is ongoing, of course, and there's never a dull moment. More than ever, I have to remember to trust God and let go of my own expectations. I do what I can to teach them and point them in the right direction, but ultimately, I have to remember that they are God's children, and He does guide them when they are at school or out with friends. I have to trust Him to help them through their own life adventure.

There is the adventure of our work and finances. Someday, God willing, I hope to write a book about that journey as well. I will just say for now that God has been in every detail, and He has provided in so many amazing ways. As we trust Him more and learn to work wisely and manage our finances better, God proves to be faithful. We have learned to give back to God more by tithing and giving to different causes, and we have seen that things always go better when we give.

Each aspect of life is an adventure of discovery. In my experience, I have learned to trust God more when encountering difficulties, and seek God's wisdom to help me see what I need to adjust on my part in order for life to work as He designed it.

There have been many challenging seasons and many seasons of breakthrough as well, and God provided the grace to walk through these seasons and learn something new and valuable every time. I have learned that God has a good plan for my life, that Jesus is gracious and loving towards me, that He has kindness towards me as well as goodness and favor. I learned that Jesus is for me, not against me, and that He accepts me as I am and forgives me. I learned that Jesus sees me as flawless and beautiful because He shines His light on me and through me.

PART TWO

12

LISTENING AND ASKING QUESTIONS

While I was driving our eleven-year-old son to school one day, I started to explain an important traffic safety rule. I think I was talking about the importance of keeping an adequate distance when crossing at school behind a car that's stopped to let the kids out, as there's the danger of the parent backing up suddenly. Well, before I could even finish my sentence, my son interrupted loudly, "I know mom! I got it! OK! I got it." He sounded really annoyed and had a mocking attitude.

I got pretty upset with the way my son reacted and his unwillingness to hear me out. I seldom use the words "shut up," but I got so worked up and I said, "Shut up and listen to me! You don't know squat!" We talked later after I calmed down and apologized for my inappropriate response. I asked him to think about why it is important to really listen and understand a matter well, instead of assuming that you already know. It could mean the difference between getting an A or an F, or it could mean serious injury and even losing your life. I think he got the picture, and I notice he has been better at listening in general.

I could go on and on about the importance of listening well: listening with the intent to understand, rather than thinking about what to say or how to get the person off your back. In the business of life, it's easy to get into a mode of turning off to things that are important, get distracted, and then get derailed.

Up to this point I've painted a picture of my life in a narrative form. I've changed the names of the people and places, but the story is true. In this part of my book, my goal is to share some insights and lessons I've learned through my life experiences. I pray that the concepts and principles I learned will be helpful either to prevent the kind of devastation I've experienced in my life, or to help bring healing and hope for someone who is currently going through terrifyingly distressing times.

In October of 2017, I was graciously gifted a ticket to High Performance Academy with Brendon Burchard. My friend was very excited about it, and she said it would prepare me to write about my journey. I took the opportunity to go and while I was there, I became more aware of the need for me to finish writing my story and publish it. One of the speakers there was a former NFL player who is now a successful author, speaker, and entrepreneur. After the seminar, I went up to talk to him. I wanted to ask him about football safety as our twelve-year old son had just started to play football. He said, "Make sure his coaches are teaching him the rugby technique, as it's lower-impact and safer."

Then I asked, "What if he gets tackled?" He smiled and answered, "Well, the whole point of the game is not to get tackled." Sure, it would be awesome if, as a team player, my son never got tackled, but is that realistic? Does that happen in real life? When considering playing football, my son expected he was going to get tackled at least a few times. He did not feel he was a failure when he did get tackled. He used the opportunity to learn how to get better at avoiding it next time. His teammates and his coach would get together after each game and talk it out. There were questions about what went down, there was some great constructive criticism, and also some great encouragement. My son had an amazing grin on his face even when his team didn't do so great. He worked through the tough questions, took the criticism seriously, and the team encouragement and the encouragement from his coaches lifted his spirits. I love to watch him and his team play.

I learned a few things as I reflected on my conversation with the former football player pro, besides good pointers for football safety. I figured, it's a pretty good idea to learn from the pros in the game of life, too.

Another thing I learned is that life is like a training field. You may get tackled a few times, but you don't have to stay down. The point is to keep getting up and fighting. As you get better at the game of life, you improve your vigilance, your speed, and your stamina; your confidence grows, and you become unstoppable. And it gets even better when you realize that life is meant to be lived as a team effort. You realize you're not alone, and you start to see the people on your team in a different light. You are able to draw on their strengths, and you share yours. And then it gets even better than that when you find out that God Himself is part of your team, and He is there to guide you, cheer you on, and help you walk out the life you've always dreamed about.

There's a story about a young man who was 12 years old when he got to go with his family to their traditional annual temple celebration. It was supposed to be a time when the high priest would go into the most sacred room, get a message from God, and share it with the people. The young man was so intrigued after the celebration that he stayed to talk to the priests and teachers. He listened to them and asked them a lot of questions, three-days-worth of questions. He forgot all about the fact that he was supposed to be on his way home with his parents. Can you guess Who I'm talking about? And can you guess what kind of questions He was asking?

I've been thinking lately about this story and the questions Jesus asked during that time at the temple. I'm thinking they were questions about God and His laws, about the meaning of life, about the coming Messiah and what the Torah said about it. The priests were amazed at the questions He was asking and were astonished at His understanding and answers as well.

One amazing thing about Jesus was that his life was all planned out beforehand, and that made me ask myself, "was my life all mapped out?" Looking back on my life, I could see some very specific indications that the course of my life was in fact known by God ahead of time, and that He was watching and guiding me through it. That gave me hope to look ahead, to keep asking questions for the next steps in my life as I experienced healing and restoration--sometimes little-by-little, and sometimes as big "Aha!" moments of clarity and vision.

I think it's extremely important to ask the right questions in life and to seek answers to the important questions of how we are created and for what purpose? How do we figure out what studies or career to pursue? How do we understand relationships, getting married and having kids? How do we know the next step to take? How do we deal with difficult situations? And more.

My hope is that this part of my book may be a springboard for reflection on some delicate questions about life. Some questions I did not consider correctly early on in life the way I would have knowing what I know now. That lack of understanding affected me deeply. I pray my readers will gain insights that would be practical and applicable, or at least gain a starting point for acquiring further understanding regarding some very important aspects of life.

Just like strengthening and protecting our physical core through physical exercises, there are things we can do to strengthen and protect our inner core to maintain balance and a sense of well-being. As I look back on my own life, I wish I had opportunities to study on some subjects as a preventive measure. A group study may have been very helpful, as it would have given other people opportunity to share their insights to bring my own blind-spots into the light. In this section of the book, I provide my readers with some of my thoughts about why my life went down the way it did, as well as provide some food for thought and reflection.

To make it easier for group study, book club or personal reflection, at the end of each chapter or main point I provide questions for meditation to help structure and encourage conversation.

My husband and I took a short trip to California a couple of years ago to attend an event and visit with family. As my husband and I were waiting to board the plane, the news came on at the terminal, and the first thing I heard was a statistic stating that suicide is the second leading cause of death for young people ages 12 through 35 in the U.S. Tears welled up in my eyes as I could understand, at least in part, the pain and temptation. I thought, *I've been there! I've been in that awful place where contemplating suicide seemed like the only option.* That was the moment I decided to go ahead and share my story in hopes that someone who is feeling like I did in my times of deep emotional and spiritual distress may see and hear that there is hope for the future.

Even if at the present time you are feeling all alone and devastated, if you hang in there and keep fighting no matter how hard it is, and keep working your way through the darkness, the lights will come back on and life will take a turn for the better.

Life can get really messy at times for various reasons, and I believe those times of turmoil are opportunities for great growth if we ask the right questions and take the right approach. My husband restores homes that have been damaged by weather, fire, or other factors. When a house is renovated, first there are varying degrees of demolition. If the wood could talk it would probably say, "This is really painful." Nails go flying, walls come down, and the dust is overwhelming. Then, little by little, not without nails and noise and more dust, you can start to see the beauty taking form until the house is finished and then, "Voila!" as my daughter loves to say, you can enjoy the fresh new look and feel, and you can finally enjoy the party.

Life is like that, too. The beauty is that the house is better, stronger, and much more enjoyable and useful after it goes through that process of renovation. So are people who go through difficult times and overcome. They become stronger, more patient, more understanding, and easier to be around. They become confident people who can then help others find their way to a beautiful and meaningful life.

Chapter 12 Questions for Reflection

☐ Who am I? Why am I here? Why does it matter?

☐ Why should I listen? To whom should I listen? How should I listen?

☐ What questions am I grappling with in my life currently?

☐ What questions should I be asking?

13

Some Lessons I've Learned

Learning My Real Value

In my youth, I used to be very judgmental and callused. I was anxious about many things, but I couldn't put my finger on why. I was very unsure of myself, but I would hide it the best I could, trying to act like I had everything together, trying to fit into the picture of the strong success-ful woman I thought I was supposed to be.

I had adopted many theories about how this life was supposed to be and had my ideas about what a Christian should be like according to my interpretation of the Bible, but I did not know the true essence of God's plans and His wonderful and mysterious ways. I realize now that His thoughts are so much higher than ours that we can't ever fully understand Him. He wouldn't be God if we did understand Him.

Truth be told, we can't ever fully understand all the why's and the how's, but we can get a much better understanding when we seek God with all honesty, not judging Him for all the problems and the injustices in the world, but realizing that He makes everything work together for good for those who make a conscious decision to trust Him.

I have learned that God's love towards us, the people He created as a reflection of Himself to enjoy the wonderful world He created, is so vast, so infinite, and so amazing. I'm learning to see people more as He does. If He gives me undeserved grace and is kind and patient with me, I can be gracious even to people who wrong me, by giving them the "benefit of the doubt," realizing that they don't necessarily fully understand how they are affecting me at the time.

Before I fell apart, I remember sitting at the table in my room one day, reading my Bible and praying, and thinking, *I really don't have a testimony.* I was born into a Christian family and knew about Jesus and the Bible from a very young age. I had decided to believe in Jesus and follow Jesus early in life. I'd heard people share some impressive stories of redemption, but when I thought about sharing my story, I couldn't come up with much at the time. I had heard my parents share about things God did, but I lacked having a personal encounter with God.

I can now say that I have seen God do so many amazing things in my life despite my failures and inadequacies. I can say that my life is an amazing testimony of God's sustaining goodness and grace. Sometimes I get so overwhelmed when I get a glimpse of how much God cares for me and how valuable I am to Him despite all my flaws and past mistakes.

Also, I know that there is a battle for my soul, and I am always tempted to choose a more comfortable way, a more popular way, a more-appealing-to-my-tastes way, or a more "logical" way, but Jesus said, "I am the way, the truth, and the life, no one comes to the Father except through me" (John 14:6). Jesus said, "Whoever loses his life for my sake shall find it" (Matthew 16:25b).

Our logic has been tainted so much by our sinful nature that what seems logical to us many times is the furthest from the truth. Pastor Mark would say, "The Kingdom of God is a backward kingdom. What seems right to us could be just the opposite." This battle takes place in the mind. I am more aware every day of the concepts I have believed over the years that kept me trapped in a mindset that was harmful to me.

We say, "Do whatever you feel right in your heart," or "What you feel in your heart you should believe, let your heart guide you." But, the Bible says things like, "The heart is deceitful and desperately wicked" (Jeremiah 17:9), and "Guard your heart with all diligence for from it come the issues of life" (Proverbs 4:23). Some Bible scholars believe the word "heart" in this passage is better translated to say "affections." "Above all else, guard your affections. For they influence everything else in your life." I believe that what happened to me came as a result of not knowing how to guard my heart. My affections were misplaced and, consequently, my emotions were deeply affected. I thank God for giving me a second chance, for giving me a new heart to start over. I pray that whoever reads this book is given the understanding to be able to recognize and avoid the things that can affect that innermost connectivity with the source of life and well-being.

What you don't know or don't accept or put off or out of mind can really hurt you. Just because many people in today's culture have accepted the concept "that truth is relative," and "what's true for you is not true for me," does not mean that absolute truth does not exist. Many scientists and philosophers when setting out to prove that God and Jesus are not real have found otherwise when looking at the evidence that is available.

The most amazing thing is that God promised to reveal Himself to anyone who seeks Him in all honesty. He loves each person He created so much and desires to dialogue and relate with each of us personally. He talks to us all the time, and we can learn how to hear Him speak to us.

Learning to Embrace Humility

It's so unpleasant to be around an arrogant person. The problem is, usually a proud person doesn't even know they are being proud and obnoxious. God says in the Bible that "He resists the proud but gives grace to the humble" (James 4:6), as well as, "pride comes before destruction"

(Proverbs 16:18).

I had a certain kind of unholy pride before all that stuff happened to me. I was filled with a sense that I knew more than others, that I knew everything about right and wrong. Of course, I acted humble and really thought I was, but I craved attention and recognition. Maybe it was because I felt so insecure and didn't know my true value.

When I think about how I acted and how I treated some people in my life, or my avoidance of certain people, I realize my own insensitivity and how it must have hurt them. Not only did it not help them, but I was the one missing out the most. I missed out on the opportunities to get to know some amazing people and learn from their experiences and wisdom.

Unhealthy pride has a way of creeping into a person's life in many ways. It can be very deceiving and destructive. The opposite of pride is humility. Though it's not necessarily popular, it is most beneficial when understood and applied correctly. My husband jokes about writing a book someday with the title, "Humility and How I Attained It," or, "The Most Humble Man and How I Trained the Other Nine."

After I was humbled so deeply, now I can say, "It is good that I was humbled because otherwise, I would have never known the depths of the love of God, the depths of His mercy and grace, the beauty of His mysterious plans, the mystery of suffering and the joy that came when I was reborn."

I discovered that God wanted me to have an abundant life; that He wanted me to excel and succeed, and that He had good plans for me and my family. Since my hope has been restored, my marriage has taken a beautiful turn, and I am able to love and respect my husband more and more daily. In turn, he has responded with more love and understanding. We spend a lot more time together and we communicate a whole lot better. We are getting to know each other in a much deeper way, and we are enjoying our wonderful children so much. Life is still a process of growth and discovery, but there is a vision for the future that makes the journey so much more enjoyable.

Hell is Real and so is Heaven

Some say there is no such thing as hell. I honestly wish that was true. I keep thinking that if the hell I experienced here on earth was so excruciating, the hell waiting for those who do not receive the grace provided by God through the sacrifice of Christ Jesus must be so immeasurably more painful, and full of regrets for all eternity. Please don't allow the pleasures of the moment to cloud your mind and prevent you from searching and finding the truth that can set you free from such a horrible destiny.

Many people don't want to consider Christianity because they think it's all about the do's and don'ts: no more parties, no more sex, and no more freedom. But what people don't know is that God is the real party animal; He created sex, and it is a wonderful thing in the context for which it was created. There is more freedom in Christ then one will ever experience in this lifetime. People don't understand that by giving themselves to God and His purposes, they are trading up and get to enjoy real freedom and fulfillment. Living life with God doesn't mean there will be no more problems or pain, but who doesn't get problems and pain anyway! Yet, going through difficulties with God beside you is what gives you strength and makes everything work out for good.

I hear a lot of talk about how we are now enlightened and, *How could people believe that there is an eternal hell?* A friend of mine said, "I can't imagine my father going anywhere except to heaven. He was such a good man." Well, if being good by our definition is good enough for God, then there would be no problem. But even Jesus Christ taught that, "No one is good except for God." If our goodness were enough, then there would be no need for Christ. Why would Jesus put Himself through the cross if there were an easier way of just living a good life? If all religions are good and all ways lead to heaven, why would God send His only Son to die such a horrible death to provide atonement? That would have been the ultimate cruelty toward his own Son if there was any other way.

Blind Spots and Foolishness

I watched a speaker on TV talk about "The Power of

Intention." He described that we just have to give in to the god inside of us, whoever that may be, and we must avoid those things that keep us from feeling good. And in fact, if someone tells you something that makes you feel bad, you should stay away from that person. I believe that's an extremely dangerous philosophy, and unfortunately, I've met many that have bought into this theory of "all spirituality is good, and it's all about the karma you make for yourself."

I lived by this theory unknowingly before the experiences I describe in this book. If someone tried to show me that I was wrong in some area of my life, I would brush them off or rationalize everything. I did not pay close attention to people who tried to correct me. Some of them did not have the right attitude, that was true, but still, when someone tells you about a blind spot, it is wisest to consider it objectively, and very dangerous to brush it off just because it doesn't feel good.

King Solomon called people like that fools. I was a fool, too, an ignorant fool, and I had to pay a very costly price for that. In fact, thinking good thoughts never helped me one bit until I discovered God's thoughts and hung on to them by faith. But thank God, I am now a "recovering" fool. We all are "fools" in that sense, I believe, until we find the true wisdom of God. There is no shame in that.

I believe a fool becomes wise when recognizing the limitation of our human understanding and takes the necessary steps to become a seeker of truth, as well as allows others to point out the blind spots so they can be corrected.

There is an ancient Hebrew tradition of celebrating the Passover to commemorate the liberation of their ancestors from slavery in Egypt and their freedom as a nation. They set the Seder table and have four cups lined up in the middle. They read or play out a story at the Seder table about four sons: one wise, one wicked, one simple, and one who didn't know to ask. All the sons are welcome at the table, and by some interpretations they represent different stages in people's lives at different levels of growth. For the wise son, there is always more room for wisdom, for the wicked, there is room for correction, for the naïve and inexperienced there is a chance to mature, and for the ignorant son, there's room to gain insight.

The father at the table is patient because he knows

"people get it when they get it," and so year after year the sons come back and are challenged to remember, to reflect, and to consider the past as they celebrate the present and prepare for the future. The Talmud teaches that man does not sin unless there has entered into him a spirit of foolishness. There is the understanding that the wicked person is wicked, evil, or rebellious because he lacks wisdom, understanding, and discernment. He would choose better if he knew better.

I see myself in all four of the sons at the Seder table at different stages in my life. I'm aware that in some aspects of my life, I could be either one of them at any point in time. It's that awareness of my need for Father's guidance and patience, and the awareness of my need for the connection that makes me seek to understand Him and desire to experience Him more and more.

It was the foolish son in me that rebelled and reaped destruction, but when, with the eyes of my heart I saw Jesus, the sacrificial Lamb that took my place, I fell in love with Him. The Father's love made it all possible, and He embraced me as His own.

Chapter 13 Questions for Reflection

- Do you know your value? How can you find your true value and worth?

- In what ways do you struggle with pride? How does a person become humble?

- What do you think about heaven and hell? Why do you think that?

- What do you think about the statement "we are all fools until we find the wisdom of God?"

14

DISCLOSURE

So, what was it that plunged me into that kind of hopelessness? I would like to take a little bit of time to talk about some of the things that happened to me as a child that contributed to the events described, and some of the conclusions I have drawn as I went through these experiences.

I felt conflicted as I began to write about my struggles in the area of sexuality. Obviously, this is a subject that is difficult to discuss. It's a very private matter, and I would prefer to keep it that way, too. Sharing puts me in a place of great vulnerability. Yet, as this is a more common struggle than I'd like to think, and if my story can be helpful to someone, I think it's all worth it. As we look around in culture and society, many people suffer even more intensely than I did as a result of sexual abuse, misplaced sexual affections, sexual addictions, addiction to pornography, and other forms of misuse of the gift of sexuality. Since I've experienced healing and restoration in this area, I want to be a voice for healing for others as well. So, here I go.

In my formative years, between ages 11 and 13, I had been repeatedly approached by a few different men who took advantage of me and took the liberty to explore me sexually. There was the time on the crowded bus when someone pinned me to the person in front of me and slipped their hand under my dress and into my under-wear. It happened so quickly, I didn't even have time to react. We were like sardines on the bus and I couldn't even turn my head to see who it was. I wiggled away, but I will never forget.

Another time, we were visiting some relatives and one aunt volunteered to take me and my siblings to the pool by the river. While in the extremely crowded pool, a friendly man came and picked me up in the water and told me he was going to teach me how to swim. Seconds later, his hand went into my bikini, (they didn't have one-piece bathing suits in Romania at the time). I must have missed the talk about what to do if some stranger approaches you or tries to touch you.

Then there was the time when a relative came to vis-it our family for a couple of days to help my dad build a special bench for the kitchen and a storage drawer. He was fun to be around, and he volunteered to take us kids for a picnic in the nearby woods. We walked to a remote side of the woods and found a little military hide-out on the side of a grass-covered mound. We tried the door and it opened. It was a small room with a bunk bed and a little table.

We played there for a few minutes and as my brother and my sister were busy there, our trusted relative called me to go explore the woods a little with him. There was a trench at a little distance in the woods, and it was covered in leaves. He said, "Let's have some fun." I guess you can imagine by now that he meant sex.

Strangely enough, as we were lying there before it all happened, three or four middle-aged people passed by on the trail behind the nearby bushes. They were dressed like farmers. They stopped and peaked over the bushes for a couple of seconds, then turned their heads to the trail and walked on.

That night after I slept for a few hours, I woke up and had the feeling there was a monster-like presence in my room. I was so terrified. I couldn't move for a while and I was careful to breathe ever so quietly. I mustered up the courage to jump up out of bed and turn on the light. When I realized there was nothing there, I went to the bathroom, went back to bed, and was able to go back to sleep.

My parents were not aware of these events, and I could never talk about them, either. Somehow there wasn't an opportunity to discuss things of that nature, and I didn't ever feel free to bring it up for discussion on my own. I remember my mother talking about the subject of sexual immorality months later and saying, "I don't know what I would do if any of you ever did anything like that." After that, I was sure I could not say anything.

During that same period, I was also tormented on occasion by terrible thoughts, especially at night. Thoughts would come to my mind, urging me to curse and blaspheme the Holy Spirit. I had heard it preached and had read it in the Bible that every sin can be forgiven except for blaspheming the Holy Spirit. I would fight these thoughts off for what seemed like hours before falling asleep. One night, I had a vision of two men that came to the foot of my bed and told me that they would hunt me down and kill me someday.

Going further back in my early childhood, probably around age 4, I had discovered masturbation and I would engage in it sometimes during nap time in preschool or at night. Although I was never told that it was wrong, I felt ashamed about it and I would always hide it. My parents never said anything about it. Either they had no clue it was happening, or thought I would grow out of it.

As I grew older, I would from time to time fall prey to this vice. It was significantly less frequent the older I got. In my high-school and college years it was more like a once-a-year type of thing. I could not discuss this issue with my parents. Somehow, I didn't feel that they would understand. Each time, I would feel so ashamed afterward and I would purpose that I would not give in to these urges anymore. When I turned 16, I made a public declaration of my decision to follow Jesus. I was determined to live in all honesty and purity, but every now and then I fell into the old temptation.

By the time I reached my 20's I had buried the memories of all the sexual abuse and related struggles, but they affected me subconsciously. I had trouble relating to people in general, and with the opposite sex in particular. I had anxieties that I could not explain. I felt ugly and inadequate, and I had developed compulsions and obsessions such as bulimia and anorexia, as well as excessive hand and face washing rituals. I developed severe acne, and although I went for professional treatment, nothing helped.

Due to my problematic eating habits, I became obsessive about exercise to prevent weight gain, and, due to the lack of adequate nutrition and excessive exercise, I had many aches and pain and cracking joints. As I learned about some of these problems in nursing school, I was able to change my habits, and I began feeling a whole lot better by the age of 24. I even felt I had been delivered of the problem with masturbation. I had prayed specifically and renounced it after I heard some teaching about the subject.

I dated different guys in my late teens and early 20's, but I could never really develop a healthy friendship due to my anxieties and feelings of inadequacy. Somehow, I always ended up driving everyone away. When I dated the man I thought I would marry, the childhood memories came back more and more, and the feelings of inadequacy intensified. I felt unfit for any man. I felt that God was telling me that I should not continue in that relationship. I wrestled with that thought for a while. But I rationalized it and said to myself, *Yes, I wasn't sexually pure in the past, but neither was he*, as I found out from our conversations. So, I made the decision to continue in the relationship.

One day a friend gave me a novel and I started to read it. It described an intriguing love story between a young Roman and a Christian woman who lived during the time after the death and resurrection of Christ. There was nothing graphic in the novel itself that I remember, but in the middle of reading it, I felt a sudden urge to masturbate. I gave into it without giving it much thought. It was as if at that moment I decided to willfully sin against God. I did not persist in the act. It lasted just a few seconds and then I stopped and thought, *What am I doing?* A flash thought came to my mind that said, *You have really done it this time, you have crossed the line*, and I even had a very vivid impression of Jesus turning His face away from me.

There was a feeling like I had taken a bite of the forbidden fruit. I quickly shook myself out of it, dismissing the experience as an illusion, and I put it out of my mind. About three months later the memory of this event started to haunt me and no matter how much I tried to get rid of it, it kept coming back stronger and stronger. It was like I had pushed the button of self-destruction and there was no going back. There was something about that one act of willful disobedience that I could not reconcile with my conscience.

At one point when the feelings of guilt became so intense, I said to God, "If You forgive me and restore me, I vow I will never marry or think about sex again." After the big breakdown, when I was finally able to talk about these things with my parents, my father relieved me of that vow and every other vow I had made in my desperation. He reassured me that I was beautiful and worthy, that God wanted me to be able to enjoy life and pleasure without guilt attached, and that included getting married if I desired.

As God began to heal me when I was set in that church, I learned a whole lot more about the reasons for my struggles. There was a pastor, speaker, and writer who was invited to speak at the church. He played an instrumental part in my healing. He explained that the enemy of our soul wants to rob men and women of their inner beauty, to distort it through: abuse, the worship of sex and unhealthy sexual practices, and the longing for the perfect body as it is depicted so much in art, movies, television, fashion, etc. Pastor Tim explained that God wants women to be His precious daughters, flowers, and princesses. But women are robbed of their bloom either through abuse or when they give their heart to men who toy with them, then leave and go looking for another flower to destroy.

Men suffer as well when sexually abused. I could see how the things that happened to me in my childhood really opened a door for the enemy to mess with me. When Pastor Tim prayed for me that I would be released from my past, I felt like a real burden lifted off my shoulder. I felt like God was embracing me again.

Chapter 14 Questions for Reflection:

☐ Unhealthy experiences in childhood can distort how we view ourselves, how we relate to others, and can contribute to ongoing emotional trauma if ignored.

☐ After reading my story in Part One, can you think of some reasons why I was not able to resolve my issues before they affected me in such a traumatic way?

☐ What are your thoughts about what caused my breakdown?

☐ Are there past experiences you may need to look at and resolve before they create havoc in your life?

15

The Heart and Mind Connection

Through all those years of inner turmoil, I never believed that I was suffering from mental illness. When I was hospitalized, my condition was labeled "inorganic brain disorder," which basically said to me, "We have no clue what we're dealing with." I think "inorganic heart dysfunction" would have been a more appropriate term. There is something in the heart that has to do with our emotional wellness.

In nursing school, we were taught that there are no cures for mental illness, and you have to keep going back for treatment to maintain some level of function. I believe this is because there is a spiritual aspect to life that needs to come into proper alignment. When the spirit is set free, we have a chance to really experience hope and life as God intended. Life then becomes a journey of real growth, and it becomes more and more fulfilling as we continue to explore the vastness of God's infinite wisdom and discover the beautiful life for which we are created.

Psychology is beginning to discover that mental illness has a lot to do with one's spiritual struggles. Doctor M. Scott Peck, MD author of *The Road Less Traveled; A New Psychology of Love, Traditional Values and Spiritual Growth* said, "Symptoms of mental illness are manifestations of grace...they notify people that their spirits are not growing and are in jeopardy."

I believe some people who are given a label of mental illness are actually suffering due to spiritual oppression. In my mom's village, there was a woman who started to have behavioral problems and was diagnosed with a form of schizophrenia. All her problems started after she visited a palm reader.

There are evil spirits that call themselves "gods," and they, too, have powers and can even do miraculous things, but their agenda is to deceive and destroy. They are very attractive, and seem like angels of light at first until they have a person trapped. I personally know a neurosurgeon who tells his story of finding God. He says he has seen the power of evil spirits growing up in Thailand in the traditions of Buddhism. He had experienced the world of evil spirits and had no problem believing in the supernatural, but when he came to know Jesus, he finally experienced real life, joy, and fulfillment.

Now, I'm perfectly aware that there is the group of mental health diseases that are caused by chemical imbalances, just like diabetes is caused by the inability of the pancreas to produce insulin. I believe those can be healed by God, too. I know of people who struggled for years with bipolar disease and were managed by medication. As they got closer to Jesus, they were healed, and successfully weaned off the medications. I have also heard of some that tried to come off the medications, but the symptoms returned, so they have to continue their medications for the rest of their life. There is no shame in that.

I am also a real believer in taking natural herbal supplements, in addition to eating a healthy diet, to make sure our bodies get the vitamins and minerals needed for optimal health. The doctor who gave my mother vitamin shots instead of antibiotics may have been motivated by greed, but I believe God used those vitamins to sustain my mom's body as it was struggling to fight off the deadly infection.

Our bodies struggle with all kinds of infirmities, and the entire creation suffers the effects of man's failure to live by God's design at the beginning of creation. I've heard many stories, though, of people who were healed physically and mentally after they decided to trust Jesus. I've also heard of a story where an entire village decided to trust Jesus and live by God's design, and as a result, not only did their families get free from devastating addictions and their effects, but their gardens started to grow produce of phenomenal size.

I attended a conference given by a very prominent psychotherapist who practices and teaches today. It was offered as a continuing education course for my nursing career. He talked about how psychotherapists need to encourage people to talk about their spiritual experiences and help them find their path. He was basically saying that there is healing in many different religions, yet the success stories he described were of people who believed in Jesus and started to see God for who He really is, not a projected image of their parents or people who have brought disappointment, suffering, and abuse in their life. He talked about how religious strain is seen in people who are unable to resolve their anger with God, for example, over the death of a child, or in those who do not espouse beliefs or church affiliations. He gave an example of a study that showed that the Judeo-Christian religion is associated with lower blood pressure, better lipid profiles, and enhanced immune functioning.

Another study showed that intercessory prayer made a great difference in the recovery of some 1,300 CCU (critical care unit) patients and 40 AIDS patients who were randomly selected and placed on intercessory prayer lists. The study subjects didn't even know that they were being prayed for, and the people that were praying were not even in close proximity to the patients. Some were in different states. Dr. Preston also talked about the negative effects of religious practices, such as legalistic and dogmatic upbringing, a "holier than thou attitude" of those in leadership, and acts of dominance or cruelty rationalized "in the Name of God."

We live in a fallen world where we struggle to try to find a balance. We are bombarded with ideas left and right, we get confused and scared; we struggle to be strong, to achieve something, to have something meaningful, and we want to leave a good legacy. We hear different messages as to how we should live and how we should discover ourselves. We try all the self-help tips and learn from the experts, the celebrities, and the talk show hosts. But no matter how hard we try, somehow, something is always missing. Life is short, time is ticking, and after a while we become more and more dissatisfied. And then there are wars, famines, and tragedies like the earthquakes, hurricanes, tornadoes, and other catastrophes, and we realize that no one is safe.

The one constant in life is that we all die. We dream, and when our dreams are dashed, we dream again. I used to think that as long as I could dream again, no matter what happened, there was still hope. Yet as I was going through those times of deepest desolation in my heart, all my dreams died and I had no more control. I could not dream again until I was set free by God to dream again.

If we are honest, we realize that this is exactly why Christ had to come: to give us a hope and a future, to give us the assurance that no matter what happens, if our hope is in Him, He works out the details and takes care of our needs even through the most tragic times. When we know Him, our dreams change, and we realize what really matters. When we live in that light, life is worth living and there are no regrets.

Chapter 15 Questions for Reflection:

- ☐ What insights do you have about the subject of spiritual health?

- ☐ Why or how may spiritual health differ from mental health?

- ☐ Why would it be important to distinguish between mental health and spiritual health? Would there be a different approach toward solutions?

16

A CRUTCH OR A FOUNDATION?

"Who needs a crutch?" some say. The question is, "Who does *not* need a crutch?" Eventually we all die, and we need to know that we will be safe. Not seeking the truth and just accepting the theories that God does not exist, that we are not tainted by sin and in need of redemption, or that life is just what we see and nothing more, is extremely dangerous, I believe.

That "dark night of the soul," as I have experienced it, was actually good for me because it forced me to seek God's help and experience the rebirth of my soul. Someone had once said, "Sometimes to find gold you have to use dynamite." I felt that way. I felt like God allowed my heart to experience that brokenness to rid me of selfishness and vain thinking and awaken me into true living. Though I was religious, I did not know Him.

My religious arrogance must have been truly nauseating to God and to the people around me sometimes.

Religion in any form eventually brings us to exhaustion, because it is our way of achieving something through our own efforts, which always falls short. But Jesus Christ brings life. It's really not about a crutch, it's about a foundation. Jesus is that solid foundation that keeps me grounded in God's gracious love.

If you believe that all beliefs are equal and all religions lead to heaven or some kind of bliss after death, I really believe you have been deceived. Christ is the only One Who defeated death through His resurrection and proved Himself to be the only begotten Son of God. He said, "I am the way, the truth, and the life. No one comes to the Father except through me" (See John 14:6). He did not say, "I am one of the many ways, one of the many relative truths out there, and one of the ways to life."

I found Lee Strobel's books helpful when I was researching more about why Jesus is the only way. Lee was an atheist journalist who embarked on a two-year journey to disprove the existence of God. In the process, he found so much evidence that God exists; He is actually a person not just some energy force out there that can be called whatever. He concluded that Jesus is exactly who He claims to be. It is wiser to really search for the truth than to risk it and go to your death without even truly looking at the evidence.

The church I attend now offers a class on Thursday nights called "Alpha." I decided to check it out one day, and I found it to be very helpful to answer many questions related to the spiritual aspect of life.

When I took a refresher course in critical care nursing, I was reminded of how complex our bodies are and how many intricate mechanisms are at work to keep all our organs functioning the way they do. It is truly a miracle that we can wake up every morning and go about our business. We take it for granted most of the time. I'm in awe of our Creator Who created us in His infinite wisdom. I am grateful that in His wisdom He provided a way, though it cost Him more than we could ever imagine, so that His creation could be redeemed from the gruesome effects of sin. It wasn't simple for Him. He provided the ultimate sacrifice. All we need to do is receive His gift.

As I went through my terrifying ordeal, I couldn't understand how a loving God would allow me to experience such deadness, such misery of the soul, such hopeless anguish. I couldn't understand why this had to happen to me, and how come He left me without even a little string of hope I could hold on to.

Yes, I did rebel in a moment of weakness, and I don't contest the fact that I did deserve to be disciplined. It just seemed so unfair that I had to suffer that kind of hell when I knew plenty of people who have done worse things, a whole lot worse, and didn't seem to be the least affected. I realize now that for each person the time comes when they must give account for what they do, but it is in God's timing, and He is the one who decides when and how to deal with each of us. I couldn't understand at the time, but I am thankful now for all of it.

Now when I get a patient who feels hopeless or who has attempted suicide, I can relate to their struggles, and I can share about the hope I have in Christ. It may take some time, but it's worth waiting and trying because something beautiful will be birthed from all the pain. Pastor Mark said in one sermon, "When you're going through hell, don't stop." I like that. It was wonderful advice at the time, and I'm grateful for those words that helped me keep going.

Our destiny is eternal. We are designed to live forever, and when we are born into the Kingdom of God by inviting Jesus Christ to become our center, life becomes beautiful, meaningful, and more and more complete. We are not promised a life without struggles and difficulties, but God helps us navigate through the difficult times.

Most recently, going through an Alpha course at church, I'm learning even more fascinating things about Jesus. I think He is like a gift that I can keep unwrapping, and I'm amazed every time because of His infinite, mind-boggling wisdom, goodness, grace, power, provision, and so many other aspects.

I used to think, *Maybe I am not chosen by God since He decided to have nothing to do with me.* But now I see more and more that God is proving me wrong. He allowed me to suffer so that He could perfect in me the true meaning of compassion, love, mercy, joy, peace, patience; all things which I understood very superficially before.

Jesus compared the process of growing with Him with the life of a vine. Jesus said, "I am the vine and you are the branches" (John 15:5), and he talked about the pruning that is done so the vine can produce more fruit. When the vine is being pruned, it does not feel good, but the end result is worth the pain. Painful experiences can help us become more loving, more understanding, more appreciative, more peaceful, and more patient.

As I struggled through those dark times, I developed a victim mentality, which affected my relationships with others. I was always the one in need, and I expected people to fulfill my needs. After all, they had it better than I did. Of course, I had more sense than to say that out loud, but that was the attitude of my heart. It was all about me.

My husband pointed that out a few times, and I thought he was just being insensitive. Through the process of my restoration, my thinking began to change as God empowered me more and more. Now I see my husband differently, and that has opened more space for understanding, more room for unconditional love, and more willingness to work through life's challenges as a team. Now I can say, like King David in Psalms 119:71, "It is good for me that I have been afflicted, that I may learn Your statutes."

My prayer is that you may allow Christ to bring the Kingdom of God into your life and experience His wonderful destiny for you. He has created you for a definite purpose. You are not just Jane or John Doe. I challenge you to find out your "Mission Impossible," and join God in the adventure of its fulfillment. If you have a hard time believing this right now, I would say to you, "Don't dismiss it." Give God a chance to reveal Himself to you. Ask Him. God can hear you anywhere you are. God promises to reveal Himself to those who seek to know Him with a sincere heart.

Chapter 16 Questions for Reflection:

- ☐ There is something about living a well-grounded life.
- ☐ What are your thoughts about religion? What do you believe about God and His involvement with humanity?
- ☐ What does it mean to have a foundation?
- ☐ What do you consider to be your foundation in life and how did you come to that conclusion?

17

Ten Practical Principles for Guarding Your Heart

As I reflected on the things that happened to me, I kept asking myself, "What could I have done differently? How could I have prevented the heartbreak and the years of torment?"

We have locks on our house doors and windows and we have locks on our cars so we can protect what's inside; keep out thieves and those who would hurt us. We install alarm systems. We put screens on our windows and doors to keep unwanted pests out of our houses. We set boundaries to keep others from invading our personal space. And while it is important to protect ourselves and each other physically and emotionally, I believe it imperative that we protect ourselves and each other spiritually. Jesus said we have three enemies: the world, the flesh, and the devil.

One way our spirit is affected is by the corrupt ways of culture and society that oppose God's design for humanity. We have to be careful what kind of people we spend time with, what books we read, what shows we watch, what music we listen to, what we view on our electronic devices, and what worldviews we adopt. All these things will help shape our future. Before Jesus ascended to heaven, He told His disciples that it is necessary for Him to go to Father God so that God's Spirit would be released to guide us and comfort us. Jesus said He gives the Holy Spirit to those who ask. The Holy Spirit then helps us distinguish our thoughts so that we can see more clearly and empowers us to make wise choices.

There is an unseen force, an enemy that seeks to pervert and destroy everything God created, especially people. This enemy influences our thoughts and beliefs. Do you find yourself thinking *I'm so ugly! No one understands me. Nobody cares about me. I'm a failure. I can't do anything right.* Where do these thoughts come from? We are not born with them. This enemy is named Satan, or called the devil, in the Bible

When we are kids, we think the best of ourselves and others, we love unconditionally, and we don't hold grudges for long. Then, as we grow and experience more in life, we pick up all kinds of ideas that we accept as truth without even giving them a second thought. Some of our beliefs have no grounding in truth. In fact, they stand between us and truth. They occupy that space, and when we hear the truth, we automatically reject it because we have no room for it. Part of guarding our heart is recognizing this enemy and learning how to differentiate our thoughts; know which ones to keep, which ones to act on, and which ones to discard or reject. And since this unseen enemy affects everyone, it is important to create healthy boundaries and develop helpful relationships.

Then there is the issue of sin. Sin keeps us from experiencing God's best for us. I heard one Bible teacher describe sin as "anything that doesn't help." We may be pretty good about guarding against "big" sins, but sometimes it's the smaller stuff that gets us trapped; things like unbelief, fear, lust, and pride. These sins are born out of accepting and tolerating wrong thinking.

In some writings, the devil is called the Lord of the

flies. I think he is more like the lord of all lies. Jesus called him a liar and the father of lies. It is those lies that clutter our thinking, and like flies that carry all kinds of disease, the lies that we accept start a process, like an infection in our spiritual life that robs us of peace, joy, and a sense of direction and purpose.

We are greatly affected by our own sins as well as the sins of people around us. Again, sin is first conceived in our thoughts, then we get to choose which action to take. The more we exercise by choosing well, the more ground is gained. When the sacrifice of Jesus is applied by faith, the past sins are erased so they no longer create a barrier to keep us from experiencing the life we are created to live. Then we are free to move forward and replace the lies with the truth.

The Bible says in Proverbs 4:23 (NKJV),

> *"Keep your heart with all diligence, For out of it*
> *spring the issues of life."*

What does that mean? How are we supposed to do that?

I've striven to organize some of the things I learned over the past twenty-some years. My hope is that my readers will gain practical and applicable insight. It's not an exhaustive list and I can't say I know all the keys to protecting one's heart, but it's a start. So, here are ten practical principles that I believe are helpful to guard your heart.

CULTIVATING FAITH

Jesus said, "Whoever believes in me, as the Scripture has said, out of his heart will flow rivers of living water" (John 7:38). Faith in Jesus is described in the Bible as a shield, a breastplate; trusting Jesus is illustrated as a helmet that protects our minds from the destructive lies of the enemy (See Ephesians 6). My journey to healing started when I decided to entrust my entire existence into His hands once again and keep standing on that decision.

There seems to be a universal law of faith. We tend to get what we believe. God says He is good and He created us and said, "This is good," and then, through the first man, Adam, sin entered the world. But God had a plan to redeem man and creation through the sacrifice of Jesus, and now through faith in Jesus, man has a chance at life again, and has all of God's wisdom and power available to tap into and fulfill God's beautiful plan for man and creation.

Imagine a beautiful world that is free of decay, free of disease, free of abuse and crime, free of lust, free of pride-- a world where love and justice are the order of the day, where all children have a loving mom and dad, and no longer live in poverty and the fear that mom and dad will split up. Imagine a world where sibling rivalry and racism are only found in legends of the past that are told to build character.

Imagine a world where animals live in harmony like pets, lions, and sheep together, no longer under the curse of sin. A world where we no longer need to worry that the next-door dog or wild coyotes or bears may attack our children.

Imagine a world free of destructive addictions that keep us and our children stuck and unable to advance toward a beautiful future.

Imagine a world free of pollution and smog, a world where technology and scientific advances are used wisely and safely for good purposes only.

Imagine a world motivated by love and goodwill. Dare to let the eyes of your mind see that world. Dare to dream again and believe that it will happen. I believe God is calling us to recreate that world with Him.

After we die, there will not be any need for faith. We will see clearly then. But now we need faith to recreate with God the world that I described above. I believe when we line up our thinking with God and unite in faith, every atom and cell will line up in perfect order and will cooperate with us to bring about the healing and the change that is needed.

I believe there will be a beautiful movement that will sweep across the planet, and every day will be more and more like Christmas Day. Remember the magic you felt when you were a child at Christmastime? Most people remember and long for that kind of life. That's why it's more painful during the holidays for some, and more people give in to hopelessness when they have lost faith in the possibility of a good and beautiful future. When I worked at the hospital, we always had more suicide attempt patients during the holidays.

When faith is cultivated, it has a chance to grow and expand beyond our wildest dreams. Faith is a powerful, motivating force that can move mountains. My friend, Joyce reminded me recently of the power of faith and encouraged me to watch some amazing discoveries in quantum physics on YouTube. There was one experiment that captured my attention: the double slit experiment. In this experiment, the particles behaved differently when observed.

When speaking about the power of faith and confession and the statement Jesus made about moving mountains by faith, Annette Capps, author of *Quantum-Faith*, says,

> "Looking at it from a surface level, it would seem a ridiculous statement that Jesus made. How is it possible that spoken words would send a mountain into the sea? For the past 27 years, it has required faith on my part to believe that my words are powerful. A recent study in the area of quantum physics, however, has convinced me that what Jesus spoke is absolute scientific fact!"[3]

Later in the article Annette remind her readers:

> "When Jesus spoke to the fig tree and said, 'No man eat fruit from thee hereafter forever,'" then that fig tree dried up from the atomic level because of His words. When He spoke to the winds and the waves, they obeyed Him. He was teaching us the undeniable Biblical principle that *things obey words.*
>
> Jesus did not demonstrate this just to prove He was the Son of God. He demonstrated it and then told his disciples that they, too, can speak words of power. He wanted us to have the revelation that we are powerful spirit beings who can speak to the moun-

tains in our life and they will obey us.

One of the reasons that some people have a hard time believing this principle is that sometimes it takes a long time for things to manifest from the unseen into this seen realm. It especially takes a long time when you dig up your seed every day to see if anything is happening yet! The seed will produce in its time if you leave it alone."

Questions for Reflection:

□ What is faith and how can one have faith?

□ What role does faith play in your life?

□ How do our words influence our circumstances?

LEARNING TO THINK THE WAY GOD THINKS

The Bible is so much more than words on paper. It is a reflection of Who God is, what He does, and how He thinks.

Reading the Bible and taking the time to reflect and study what God is saying through the Bible is a very important key. Since the battle is in the mind, God wants us to renew our minds, to think the way He does, to see ourselves and our circumstances from His perspective, to understand His worldview.

The words of the Bible are powerful. They sure cut to the core of my being during those times of distress in my life. But the words of the Bible also became the source of healing and empowerment and hope for me.

Sometimes when I read the Bible, God will bring into focus a passage in a new way that applies to my situation or gives me a clue as to what the solution might be. It's truly energizing when that happens.

The Bible says God's thoughts are higher than our thoughts. There is an infinite amount of wisdom that is contained in the Bible, and God reveals it to us in bite-sizes when He sees fit. I am so amazed at His wisdom, and now when I look at my situation and it seems hopeless, I remind myself that He is infinitely bigger than how I see my situation and how I feel about it currently. From God's perspective, the puzzle piece of my current situation may be the most beautiful part of the puzzle when it gets completed. It helps me redirect my thoughts and trust Him with the outcome.

It seems to me that there is no limit to the depth of understanding one can get out of the Bible. It is believed to be the best-selling book of all time, year after year. I find that when I spend time reading and studying the Bible in the mornings, as I tune in to what God is saying to me personally through what I'm reading, I am inspired, my mind is more focused, my attitude gets adjusted, and I'm able to accomplish more.

Questions for Reflection:

☐ Can we know how God thinks?

☐ How can we learn to think God's way?

☐ Why is studying the Bible important? How do I go about studying the Bible?

GO LOW - PRACTICING HUMILITY

Proverbs 3:5-6 (NKJV) says,

> *"Trust in the LORD with all your heart, And lean not on your own understanding; in all your ways acknowledge Him, and He shall direct your paths."*

It takes having a humble heart to always question everything you think, say or do, and to double-check yourself through God's filter. It means you have to have a teachable heart, a heart that is willing to grow in understanding perpetually, a heart that is willing to say, *I don't know everything, and I must always be cautious not to be steered wrong by my emotions or my peers, my own opinions, or the opinions of others. I must know the truth, I must know what God has to say about a matter.*

Humility helps us focus on the fact that we are God's creation, and compared to God we are like sand. It helps us to stay focused on true priorities in day-to-day life and protects us from pride, which leads to destruction. A person who has developed an attitude of humility will take time to listen well without preconceived assumptions. A humble person will look for the value in a person rather than focus on their flaws, and will find a way to deal with flaws when necessary in a caring way, having the other person's best interest in mind.

A humble person will be teachable, admit wrongdoing quickly, and be open to input and feedback. A humble person is hard to offend.

There is much to be said about humility and its many facets. Here are some quotes I found on this subject of humility that may be helpful:

> "The best protection one can have from the devil and his schemes is a humble heart." - Jonathan Edwards

> "As long as you are proud you cannot know God. A proud man is always looking down on thing and people: and, of course, as long as you are looking down you cannot see something that is above you." -C.S. Lewis[4]

Humility is a mindset, as well as a heart attitude. We need to be intentional about setting our minds to seek and develop a heart of humility. Humility helps us become more authentic and helps us develop good connections with people.

Jon Bloom stated in an online article on Desiring God,

> "Humility is not a human emotion or demeanor; it's simply the lack of pretense. Humility is the acceptance and honest confession of what is actually true."[5]

False humility is thinking less of ourselves than who we are and who we are becoming. Bloom ends his article with the exhortation,

> "Let us also lay aside every weight and prideful sin that makes us timid to hold ourselves up as examples of Christ-likeness (Hebrews 12:1). Such timidity often has its root, not in god-

ly humility, but in pride — pride that wants to conceal our tolerated disobedience and fleshly indulgence, or pride that fears what others think of us. Let us with humble honesty confess our sinful failings in order to be increasingly free of them, and our capacity limitations in order to benefit more from others' gifts. But let us also be humble and honest enough to point to the grace of Christ in us that is meant to help others walk in a manner worthy of the Lord."[6]

Humility is a lifelong pursuit, as are all aspects of wisdom. Many books have been written about humility, and the more you read about humility, the more areas you can identify where you can grow in humility. You can always go lower no matter how humble you think you are, and the lower you go, the better you will feel.

Questions for Reflection:

- ☐ What is humility?
- ☐ What can we do to develop an attitude of genuine humility?
- ☐ Why is pride so bad, and how can we clear our hearts of pride?

PRACTICING GRATITUDE AS A LIFESTYLE

Like humility, gratitude helps keep us focused on the important things in life. It helps keep us centered. Gratitude, first and foremost, means recognizing the source of all good things and showing our appreciation. Gratitude does not always come naturally. It takes intentionality on our part.

The greatest breakthrough in my life came after I decided to worship God with all my being no matter how I felt. I did this at church, at home, and in my car several times a day. I would put a worship CD on and would just sing along, raising my hands, sometimes dancing or kneeling to honor God. When my circumstances were especially difficult, I kept worshiping no matter what things looked like. My circumstances did not necessarily change right away, but the way I perceived them and the way they affected me changed. Harsh words from others did not bother me as much, and my feelings toward people and my circumstances changed.

I've seen something at work in me. At first, I fought for "my rights," and I sought after them. I sought after "my right" to be beautiful, fulfilled, dignified, loved; I sought after my right to privacy, my right to own certain things, my right to be treated with respect, etc. When I felt like I was robbed of a sense of dignity and inner beauty, and my right to be free and complete was gone, I thought, *They weren't my rights anyway, because according to the justice of God my only right is to perish in hell.* I considered it a privilege that I could breathe, that I was not in excruciating pain, that I had a roof over my head and food from day to day, and that I had people who cared about me. Then I started to be thankful for the hard things in life because I began to see how they helped shape me. I started to thank God for those who did not treat me the way I wanted to be treated, or needed to be treated, and I asked God for practical ways I could show them my love. When I started to do this, the things I considered rights before were given to me without my asking. But now I see them as privileges, and they bring me so much joy and fulfillment.

Jesus set the first example. He did not demand His right to privacy, to a room of His own with air conditioning and heating, with comfortable furniture, with room service, not even to His right to pleasure in a sexual relationship. Instead, He allowed His private space to be invaded; He was beaten, spit upon, despised, and crucified. Yet after His death and resurrection, He inherited everything as His privilege. And He doesn't even hog it for Himself – that brings Him no pleasure. He shares it with all of us who follow in His footsteps and give up our "rights." When we trust Him completely and die to ourselves, our resurrected hearts and transformed minds experience the real joy of His inheritance that includes much more than we could ever wish for.

Much has been written about the importance of gratitude. I know from my own life that on days when I think about the good things I am blessed to have, I feel more energetic and I can accomplish more. Two psychologists, Dr. Robert A. Emmons of the University of California, Davis, and Dr. Michael E. McCullough of the University of Miami, found through one study that people who wrote daily about things they were grateful for were more optimistic and felt better about their lives. The grateful group also exercised more and had fewer visits to physicians than those who focused on sources of aggravation.[7]

It is important to exercise gratitude towards God and the people in your life, and to let them know verbally, in writing, or other creative ways. Keeping a gratitude journal is also helpful, as you can look back and be reminded of the things you are grateful for in difficult times when it's hard to express gratitude.

Questions for Reflection:

☐ What are three things you are grateful for today?

☐ Should one be grateful to God or just grateful in general, and why?

☐ What is worship? What role does it play in your life? What are some ways you are created to worship God?

CULTIVATING LIFESTYLE OF LEARNING AND SERVING

Life is a continuum of learning opportunities, like a training field. Henry Ford said, "Anyone who stops learning is old, whether at twenty or eighty. Anyone who keeps learning stays young." If you have read my book to this point, you are definitely young. And though you may get some wrinkles over time, if you keep learning and searching, you will be young and beautiful forever.

Learning is also helpful for emotional healing and well-being. Jesus said, "you shall know the truth and the truth shall set you free" (John 8:32 ESV).

We learn many different ways. We learn through our senses, through life experiences, through our successes and failures, and we learn a lot through different people in our lives. Growing up, we learn from our parents, grandparents, relatives, babysitters, teachers, and peers. We learn from reading books, magazines, and listening to or watching all types of broadcasts. And then there is the idea of learning through a mentor or a coach.

Wikipedia describes mentorship as "a relationship in which a more experienced or more knowledgeable person helps to guide a less experienced or less knowledgeable person. The mentor may be older or younger than the person being mentored, but he or she must have a certain area of expertise. It is a learning and development partnership between someone with vast experience and someone who wants to learn." Wikipedia further states that this process "entails communication, usually face to face and during a sustained period of time, between a person who is perceived to have a greater relevant knowledge, wisdom, or experience (the mentor) and a person who is perceived to have less (the protégé)."[8]

Jesus modeled a lifestyle of dependence on God, The Father, for instruction in everything He did. Then, after He was tempted multiple times and overcame the temptations, Jesus went on to choose twelve people to mentor in order that they in turn would train others. In some Bible translations this process is referred to as discipleship.

When I looked up the meaning of "discipleship" in different resources, I found that it involved more than just mentoring. I saw that in ancient times, disciples learned by imitating the teacher's entire way of life and not just by remembering the spoken words of the teacher. I learned that healthy discipleship involves building relationships that feature love, commitment, authenticity, vulnerability, accountability, and intentionality.

A good disciple had the qualities of being faithful, available, and teachable. That quality of being teachable is vitally important. It means being open to receive instruction and correction when needed, assuming good will and good intent.

In our days, we often look up to professionals, especially in the sports fields. We call them pros. The term is not necessarily limited to sports, though in other fields, the term expert is used more often. It is considered a great honor to have opportunities to learn from the pros, the experts. Their words have more weight and credibility. Having a pro for a coach is definitely more desirable if it is a possibility. It's like learning from the best, the people who have achieved recognition in their field and have demonstrated a high level of expertise. I like using the term "pro" when it comes to coaching, as life is likened in the Bible to a race that is worth running well. (Hebrews 12:1)

Jesus modeled a way of life in which He associated Himself closely with those He discipled. He ate with them, traveled with them, and spent a lot of time with them. It was a nurturing lifestyle of friendship, compassion, and servitude. His disciples saw how He healed people and released them from oppression, how He went up to the mountain at night to pray and spent time with God, The Father, and become refreshed and empowered by His Pro. They saw how He prayed and struggled to accept the will of God for the cross, and how He overcame and was enabled to endure the cross for the good of His friends and all who would believe.

Then, when Jesus was resurrected from the dead, He met with His disciples repeatedly and prepared them for His ascension and for the releasing of His Spirit that would empower His disciples to live extraordinary lives that impacted and continue to impact the entire planet.

I like to think of Jesus as The Pro of all time, the One who engaged in the game of life with determination, purpose, and most of all, with love.

I believe we are all created to live a life of exchange, to learn from the pros and become pros that impact others. When we entrust ourselves to the discipleship process of the greatest of all pros, Jesus Christ, as well as engage, intentionally and consistently, in this process with others who are further along in their training, we will live lives that have great impact. Each human being is so unique and gifted, and each of us have a lot to contribute to the world around us.

When we overcome difficulties in our own lives, we grow in character and strength. Difficulties have a way of equipping us to be an encouragement to those who face similar difficulties and need our support. When facing difficulties, we can choose to withdraw and isolate, or we can choose to look for opportunities and engage in the fight to overcome.

There were times in my life when I went forward for prayer at church every time the opportunity was there, sometimes every Sunday after the service for months and months. Each time, God met me there through the people who were available to pray, and sometimes cry with me.

There were times of great discouragement, and the home group through church was a lifeline to me. They were the pros that taught me invaluable lessons in those seasons of my life.

I will mention some of the pros that have walked with me through my process so far in the Acknowledgments section of this book, and I encourage you to explore your own opportunities for growth so that you may accomplish your dreams as you discover your beautiful destiny. I'd like to encourage you, as well, to start writing your own journey if you have not already done so, as you take advantage of the learning and discipleship opportunities that God sends your way, so that you may experience life to the fullest and leave a rich legacy for those who are in your sphere of influence, those who come after you, and those who are yet to be born.

Questions for Reflection:

□ What is discipleship?

□ Is discipleship/coaching/mentoring necessary, and why?

□ What opportunities for discipleship/mentorship/coaching are available to you right now?

PERSEVERANCE THROUGH VULNERABILITY

I believe we all have secret battles, and winning one battle doesn't mean we have won the war. After that terrible breakdown in my life, I reflected on how I had let my guard down after I experienced freedom in the area of sexual purity in my life, and I was not careful to set up a way to guard my heart for the future. If we struggle with certain temptations and we gain ground, or we feel like we have conquered in an area of life, we must be very careful not to think we are out of the woods. Temptation comes repeatedly and at times when we are most vulnerable. We are tempted in our mind first, and that temptation starts a process of arousing our emotions and governing our behavior.

We've got to stop the process right where it starts. The minute we get a thought, we've got to filter it, and if it doesn't line up with God's will, we must reject it and immediately replace it by refocusing our mind on something that is true, noble, right, pure, and honorable (Philippians 4:8).

It is good to pray in the mornings, "God, I give you my thoughts in exchange for Your thoughts. Please help me so that I don't become deceived and overcome by wrong thoughts that lead to wrong behavior."

It's also helpful to develop a relationship of accountability with a trusted friend. By sharing our struggles with transparency, we allow another person to bring insight and support. Sometimes, a support group is more efficient. Hiding our struggles because of pride, shame, or fear will only place us at more risk. A soldier never goes to war alone. He goes to war against the army of the enemy with his regimen. This way, he is stronger and increases his chances of staying alive and winning.

Rick Warren, in his book *The Purpose Driven Life*, says,

> "Satan wants you to think that your sin and temptation are unique, so you must keep them a secret. The truth is we're all in the same boat. We all fight the same temptations, and "all of us have sinned." Millions have felt what you're feeling and have faced the same struggles you're facing right now. The reason we hide our faults is pride. We want others to think we have everything "under control." The truth is that whatever you can't talk about is already out of control in your life: problems with your finances, marriage, kids, thoughts, sexuality, secret habits, or anything else. If you could handle it on your own, you would have already done so. Willpower and personal resolutions aren't enough."[9]

There is a lot of freedom to be gained through transparency and authenticity. Sharing helps us stay humble, while at the same time brings us closer together. Jesus said, "The truth will set you free" (John 8:32). When you release your secret by confession, your secret loses its power over you.

Through all that has transpired in my life, I have learned something about the importance of sharing our experiences with others. There is so much power in sharing. I believe we are created to share just like Jesus shared His life. He surrounded Himself with a few close friends and shared life with them. He shared with the multitudes also as He became known.

My greatest breakdown happened at a time when I was isolated and unprotected because there were things in my life I had not been able to share over a long period of time. I was isolated in my mind, which led me down a path of isolation in my relationships within my family and community.

My greatest breakthroughs came through sharing my thoughts and feelings with those I felt I could trust and receiving by faith what they had to share with me. This process was repeated over and over in my life, whether I was sharing with a friend over coffee, responding to an altar call at church and asking for prayer, or deciding to participate in a small group.

Questions for Reflection:

☐ What is vulnerability?

☐ Do you struggle with being vulnerable?

☐ Can you think of an area of your life where you need to work on becoming vulnerable in order to facilitate breakthrough?

DEVELOPING OUR SPIRITUAL SENSES – SIGHT, HEARING, and OTHERS

Physical eyesight is so useful. I sure can appreciate the gift of eyesight more now that I've started to need glasses for reading smaller print. Spiritual eyesight is something more valuable even than physical eyesight. This is a sense that can be developed and exercised when we connect with God by faith. In my experience, when my spirit was in distress, even my physical eyesight was affected. I remembered going on hikes and enjoying the magnificent sights prior to my breakdown. That sense of awe and wonder that the beauty of the mountains, rivers, and flowers inspired in me vanished during those dark years until there was a breakthrough. When I felt God had forgiven me, I was able to see and enjoy life, people, and nature in a whole new way. There is a spiritual light that is released when the heart is purified by God.

Recently, I felt like I really blew it again. I was dishonest in a situation, and I felt like I had crossed that line of grace again. My life energy was drained again, making it difficult to focus on my home life and my work. I had done what I could to make things right, but I still felt terrible. I was praying and asking God to show me if there was still hope for me because I felt like a total failure again, and I felt like I could not finish writing my book.

As I was praying, God gave me a picture that encouraged me very much. I saw my favorite shoes thrown about on the floor, but right in front of me, there was a beautiful pair of winter boots. They looked classy, like a pair of ice-skating boots, but they had a rim of soft plushy material at the top. The boots looked warm, comfortable, and practical. It was like God was telling me that He had grace for me, and an assignment to walk out still. Through that picture, I felt God was saying to me that there will continue to be difficulties, and my feelings will not necessarily be warm and cozy all the time, but He has made preparations to help me get through the tough times ahead.

Sometimes, as I read the Bible, I see a concept in a whole new way, or I see how it applies practically to a specific situation I'm dealing with. That is also an example of spiritual eyesight.

Oswald Chambers, an early twentieth-century evangelist, and teacher, best known for the devotional *My Utmost for His Highest*, wrote,

> "Remember that spiritual vision depends on our character— it is "the pure in heart" who "see God." God makes us pure by an act of His sovereign grace, but we still have something that we must carefully watch. It is through our bodily life coming in contact with other people and other points of view that we tend to become tarnished. Not only must our "inner sanctuary" be kept right with

God but also the "outer courts" must be
brought into perfect harmony with the
purity God gives us through His grace.
Our spiritual vision and understanding
are immediately blurred when our "outer court" is stained. If we want to maintain personal intimacy with the Lord
Jesus Christ, it will mean refusing to do
or even think certain things. And some
things that are acceptable to others will
become unacceptable for us.[10]

Another sense is being able to hear with your spirit. This sense becomes clearer when you are able to quiet yourself, remove distractions, and remove yourself
from noise. You can then practice listening for the voice
of God, and practice distinguishing God's voice from all
other voices. As with spiritual eyesight, there needs to be
a spiritual cleansing for the sense of spiritual hearing to be
awakened.

I was asking Jesus some specific questions during a
prayer session I had scheduled with a couple of trusted
women from church. I was encouraged to think about
traumatic things that happened to me in the past, to see
if there were people I still needed to forgive and release.
I was encouraged to ask specific questions and just listen
for His answer. I was overwhelmed to hear simple yet profound answers that were so helpful to lift me out of the
gloom I was experiencing. Jesus reminded me that I had
not forgiven some people completely. Then He assured me
that He was present with me during the times of distress
and was training me to trust Him. He also reassured me
of His light that was being purified in me so that others
would be restored also in the future.

Life can feel so mundane and meaningless at times, but
when we take the time to reflect and listen to the voice of
God, we get a broader perspective, we see new possibilities, and we are encouraged and inspired. My day always
goes smoother and I get a lot more done when I take time
in the morning to pray and quiet my heart and listen.

God also talks to people through dreams and visions.
The Bible says that in the last days people will have dreams
and visions because the Holy Spirit will be released (Acts

2:17). My mother had dreams like that throughout her life. She had dreams that came true many times as I was growing up.

My mom had a dream in 1989. In her dream, the three of us kids that are closer in age were playing by a pond near a forest. There was a preacher who was climbing a mountain, and many were following him, but we decided to stay and play by the pond. And as night was falling, she could hear the wolves howling from the forest. I remembered this dream sometimes, but I didn't really know what it meant. I did not give it too much importance prior to my breakdown. Later, I realized how that dream was supposed to be a warning, but as I lacked insight at the time, I did not see the warning signs along the way and did not know how to avoid the dangers of what was up ahead. The dream found its fulfillment and I barely made it. The wolves of despair almost took me out, but did it have to be that way? I believe that much of my inner turmoil could have been prevented if I would have understood and interpreted that dream correctly.

Another time, my mom had a dream that I was followed by a wolf. I misinterpreted that dream, too, thinking it was about a certain person. Now, I realize, it was about a wrong mindset pattern. We can never forget that our enemy is after our mind and after our heart. He knows where your weakness is, and he waits to catch you off guard.

We've got to recognize our weaknesses, know how to guard ourselves, and know when we are more vulnerable, so we can position ourselves and stay alert and in tune with our Creator. This is easier when we are willing to talk things through with people who have more experience than us in the spiritual realm to help us see our blind spots. A good coach can help identify areas that need work and provide helpful insight.

Questions for Reflection:

- ☐ What is your experience with spiritual senses?
- ☐ Have you noticed through which senses you discern God communicating to you? (Some examples are: dreams, visions, pictures, sounds, impressions, feelings, smell)
- ☐ What resources are you using to develop your spiri-

tual senses?

THE PRINCIPLE OF DIVINE PLACEMENT INTO A HEALTHY COMMUNITY

Humans are created to be relational. We are familiar with the saying, "No man is an island," and it is well-known that isolation is destructive, yet it's easy to become isolated. Throughout life, we are involved in different types of communities. Our family is our first model of community. Schools are another form of community. Now, with all the technology, there are countless online communities in which one can be engaged.

The church is a form of community designed by God for encouragement, support, and spiritual growth. One might think of the church as a spiritual family. In the Bible, the church community is compared to the human body, each member working together to benefit the whole. In God's Kingdom, Jesus is the Founder and Leader (the Head), and we – the church universal, the people – are His Body, each playing a vital role which benefits not only the person, but the whole community.

I believe God has a place for each person within a healthy church community where one can receive and give encouragement and experience personal and spiritual growth and healing when needed. It's important to understand what church is the right one for you. If you are in the right church, you will grow and mature spiritually and you will be encouraged. You will find that you can serve others within that community and nurture others to grow and mature, so, in turn, they can do the same with their lives. It's so beautiful and fulfilling when you are in the right place with the right people. It will feel awkward and draining when you are not in the right place. Sometimes, it's a matter of patience, because you may just need time to find the right role within that community.

We find in the Bible an analogy that we are like trees that are planted and that are to take root downward and produce fruit upward (Psalm 1:3; Jeremiah 17:8). On one hand, I know that passage refers to God being our Source, but I also believe it refers to being connected in a good church community. A guest pastor at my church once said something that stuck with me, "There are many different kinds of people. People who are like the garden variety tree that go to a church, but get offended easily because 'the pastor didn't make me feel good or didn't pay attention to me that Sunday,' or other reasons. So, they get themselves uprooted and go to a different church where after a while something offends them, and they leave again to find a better place, or stop attending at all."

Positioning our heart to be open to what God is saying to us through other people in our lives is very important. When we go to church or we talk to people, we need to posture our heart to receive instruction, even criticism and correction, rather than allow our pride to interfere with our ability to see our blind spots.

I've made it my life goal to be unoffendable and always give a person the benefit that their intentions are good, even if their attitudes and words seem to be saying otherwise. I value community and seek opportunities to be involved in some kind of community activity at least twice a week.

Questions for Reflection

- ☐ Are you actively involved in a church community? What other types of community can you be involved in so you can grow in this aspect in your life?

- ☐ If you believe you're in the right place, are you serving in the right role there?

- ☐ How can you find the right community if you are not yet part of one?

PRAYER AND FASTING

I learned about prayer and fasting at an early age. My grandparents would fast for 24 hours a couple of times a month, at least. Sometimes Grandpa would fast for one week straight, and only eat one small meal after sundown each day. One day Grandpa decided we could participate as kids and not eat until lunchtime. We started reading the *Pilgrim's Progress* by John Bunyan together in Romanian, and he asked us to translate each sentence as he read it to Grandma who could only understand Hungarian. It was a fun exercise for us. We felt we were doing something valuable and interesting, while sacrificing our appetites to honor God in a special way for a few hours.

Before the soul-tearing experience, I fasted a few days now and then, but I wish I had made it a habit to fast and pray regularly, especially when I got into that dating-courting-more-like-dorting relationship ("dorting" a made-up word one of the pastors at my church used, referring to a mixture between dating and courting). Hindsight is 20/20, right? I'm thinking fasting would have probably been helpful.

Fasting is a denial of something of the flesh in order to focus on worshiping God and seeking a closer relationship with God through prayer. It's a way of saying to God that knowing Him is more important than anything in this life. It also opens up more time for reflection and helps develop our spiritual senses.

Many great leaders who had a powerful impact in Christian history practiced fasting regularly, and especially when they felt less power in their ministry. I've been learning recently how fasting helps you control your appetites, rather than allowing the appetites to control you.

On and off through my entire life, I heard about the benefits of fasting. I read studies on fasting, and more and more research has been done even more recently about the amazing benefits of fasting on a regular basis.

Fasting has physical and spiritual benefits. Physically, fasting helps us curb our appetites, which we all know can run rampant, get out of hand, and affect our overall physical health, as well as the way we feel from day to day.

When I fast regularly, I find that I have an easier time maintaining a healthy weight, I feel more energy, and my blood pressure and heart rate are better. Fasting affects my mood and focus, as well, in a positive way, and I find myself able to accomplish more.

In addition to fasting from food or maybe in place of fasting from food at times, I believe it is important to fast from things that feed our minds, such as books, media, and entertainment and allow God to cleanse things from our minds that are harmful to our well-being.

Fasting is one of the best ways to detox your body and mind, and when practiced regularly with prayer, it's a great prescription for growth and breakthrough.

Questions for Reflection:

- How is prayer and fasting beneficial?
- How much time do you devote to prayer and fasting?
- What kind of fasting is God calling you to do right now?
- What resources can you use to help you grow in this vital area of your life?

UNDERSTANDING SEXUALITY

Finally, I would like to tackle the subject of sexuality a little bit, as it was a point of such struggle for me. I struggled more at the subconscious level at first, which then grew into a full-blown breakdown in the prime of my life. If you are a young person, this is an area where you may want to pay close attention.

There is something about our sexuality that is sacred and needs to be protected. Our sexuality is created by God, and it is intended to be beautiful, pure, and innocent. Sex was designed to be a celebration of a beautiful union between a man and a woman within the loving relationship of marriage. Sexuality is connected to the core of our being.

When sin entered the perfect world God created, sexual sin was born also. Love was tainted by lust, guilt, shame, blame, and every other sin. Being naked did not affect Adam and Eve in the Garden of Eden before they sinned. They were like innocent children. After they sinned, they felt shame and had to cover their bodies. Sin affected how they saw each other, especially as it related to their sexuality, and they hid. Because of their sin, they had to leave the garden.

God wanted to make sure that Adam and Eve would not eat of the Tree of Life after they had pushed the self-destruct button, because then they would have lived forever in that state of continuous pain and decay. God provided clothes for them to cover their nakedness. Then God provided a way for them to be cleansed of their sin through animal sacrifices until Jesus became the ultimate sacrifice to atone for the sin of humanity. Through Jesus, God made it possible for innocence to be restored to the human soul no matter how deep the devastation.

An interesting thing happened to me during my dating with the guy I briefly mentioned, before all hell broke loose. I was visiting him at his place in Sacramento, and as we were walking out of his room, the picture of me that he had propped against the wall on a little table fell on the floor. He saw the picture fall and he said, "Your picture fell down," but he did not proceed to pick it up. "It's just a picture," I said to myself, but later I thought, *This should have been a sign to me that he did not really care all that much about me.* As I thought more about that relationship, more things came to mind that were clear signs that the man did not really have my best interest in mind.

I did not really want a dating relationship at that time. I had learned some things about courtship and I wanted that kind of relationship because I wanted to be safe and do the right thing. Yet what I had gotten into was more like "dorting." That was dangerous for me because I was so vulnerable due to the tension between my unresolved past experiences and my desire to do the right thing.

I didn't want to get into kissing and physical intimacy with him early into the relationship. I wanted to save that for marriage. I wanted to know him well first, and I had mentioned that to him, but he did not honor my wish. Funny that he kissed me only once shortly after I had shared my wish. The kiss was fairly intense, and he even bit my lower lip slightly. The problem was not necessarily the kiss. The problem was that he dishonored my desire.

After that he did not kiss me again, so I thought, *Well everybody makes mistakes,* yet I believe that it was enough to tip me over into the old sinful pattern of thinking lustful thoughts and opened a door for the ultimate temptation for me where I was most vulnerable at the time. Looking back it was like the sting of the devil himself, or one of his demons, working in a conniving way through that young man.

Through my experience, I learned that when innocence is lost through any form of sexual perversion, something breaks down at the core. The Bible distinguishes sexual sin from other sins. I know to a lot of people what I'm writing about sounds so crazy, living in a culture that idolizes sex and encourages exploring your sexuality. Yet for a woman, especially, the soul is a fragile thing and toying with her emotions through sensual physical contact outside of the commitment of marriage can be very harmful. Men are affected, also, by sexual perversion in different ways. This is a difficult and complex subject to unwrap and deal with, but I believe it is necessary.

I believe there is a connection between our need to feel loved and our sexuality. When something happens and distorts that connection in our perception, we experience feelings of insecurity which are basically different forms of fear. Fear and perfect love can't mix. The Bible says, "... perfect love casts out fear...." (1 John 4:18 NKJV) But perfect love is only possible in the security of God's love. Much of what we label as love is distorted and dysfunctional, and becomes good ground for fear to take root and cause problems.

As a nurse, I have seen many patients who suffer greatly because of something that happened to them through some form of breakdown in a love relationship. Also, just about every suicide or suicide-attempt case I have seen as a nurse, was related, somehow with some form of breakdown in a love relationship, even if it was only perceived in the person's mind. When I became convinced of God's unconditional love for me and His good plans for my life, I no longer felt I had to depend on others to feel complete.

I grew up in a church that encouraged sexual purity, yet the guys in that church were either too holy to even look at a woman let alone talk to her, and the others just wanted to corner you, touch you, and kiss you as soon as they got a chance. Neither one appealed to me. There was no balance, and I felt out of place. I felt insecure and fearful.

I've seen a great thing happening in some church communities now. There's instruction for the guys to learn to understand a woman's vulnerabilities, and learn to be true brothers that interact on a real friendship level with the girls without pressures for physical contact. The girls are put at ease, they don't feel they have to perform for the guys, so they are free to be real and be true sisters. If men and women become confident in their worth and value, they will experience more freedom to relate to each other in healthy ways. When loving each other includes the respect for each other's sexual wholeness as well during dating or courtship, then when the couples get married, there can be satisfaction without guilt and shame.

I pray that my book will be a call for men and women

to be restorers and protectors of each others' sexual purity. I pray they desire to keep each other accountable, to help each other grow and mature in their devotion to Christ, and to be reformers of a culture that is blinded by lust and sexual perversion. I pray that men will learn to honor women as daughters, flowers, and princesses, regardless of their past, in order that there may be restoration. I pray that women will learn their true identity in Christ, and realize that when they commit their life to Christ, they start with a clean slate and become worthy to love and be loved. What happened in the past no longer has to dictate how we view the future and how we relate to life. Our past does not have to limit what we can accomplish.

Questions for Reflection:

- ☐ What kinds of things influence the way we view our sexuality?
- ☐ How can we protect our sexuality?
- ☐ What resources are available to help you navigate this issue in a healthy way?

Additional Thoughts for Reflection:

Protecting the heart is multi-faceted and we can never be too careful. Lets recap.

- ☐ What is the first thing that comes to mind regarding the subject of guarding the heart?
- ☐ Why is it important to guard your heart?
- ☐ What principles stand out to you as you think about what you read in this chapter?

18

A LIFE GUIDED BY THE SPIRIT OF GOD

Finally, no matter how much knowledge we gather, if we don't have the constant guidance of the Holy Spirit, a life of faith is still impossible. Jesus promised to send His Spirit to comfort us and guide us. Knowledge can breed pride, and pride blinds us to the Spirit of the ways of God. But the Spirit of God guides us in wisdom, which helps us apply knowledge the right way and at the right time. We need to learn how to fine tune our spiritual senses to the presence of God's Spirit within us, so that we can hear God and see everything through God's perspective.

Before ascending to heaven, Jesus told His disciples that He had to go to the Father so that He could send Holy Spirit, the Spirit of truth, to comfort and guide us. Jesus' mission was completed and now it was time for the Holy Spirit era to begin--a time when the Spirit of God would connect each person that is reconciled to God by faith in the sacrifice of Jesus, to God. When we come to faith in Christ, Holy Spirit is released to renew us from the inside out. He lives in our hearts and speaks to us from there. His strength is available to us from within us, and we can learn to be guided by Him. We have to learn how to differentiate the voice of the Holy Spirit in us from the other voices that compete for our attention and our affection.

There are many teachings and writings about how to hear the voice of God and how to live a life that is guided by the Spirit of God. There are many teachers that have great understanding and a lot of experience. My goal in this book is not to provide a lot of information, but to shed some light on the subject, and to share some of my own thoughts and experiences related to this vast topic.

As I have mentioned, there was one specific moment in my life when I responded to an impulse in a way that was difficult for my mind and my heart to reconcile. In my quest to find answers, I have done a lot of reflecting on the events that transpired in my life to see what contributed to my inability to withstand that temptation. My conclusion was that I had not exercised enough in hearing and responding to the voice of God. I made many decisions based on my own logic, reasoning, and understanding of right and wrong. I responded a lot out of my insecurities and fears. I could not be guided and comforted by the Spirit of God when I was being guided by fear, judgment, insecurity, and condemnation related to my unresolved past.

While my thoughts and my feelings condemned me, I felt there was no hope.

Pastor Bill Johnson stated in one sermon,

> "The challenge with our faith is not our inability to hear God's voice. The challenge of our faith is our willingness to hear other voices. There are so many opinions, ideas, and ideologies that are all competing for our attention and ultimately our affection."

My friend, Tyler Frick, talks about how evil spirits may also be part of that inner conversation. Tyler is a pastor and teacher who came to faith in Christ after being involved in witchcraft, as he was exposed to it from an early age. He wrote a book called Mind Traffic. In his book, Tyler invites you to picture your mind as a busy intersection where,

> "the cars are actually thoughts, reasonings, desires, and utterances from spiritual beings.
>
> .... we are surrounded by spiritual entities, spiritual beings located in second and third heaven, functioning around us for good (to help us), and for bad (to harm us).
>
> One of the ways we can learn to understand these communications is to begin to learn how to realize what's actually happening around us from moment to moment. Why do we think random thoughts? Are they random? Do angels try to talk to us? Do they try to minister to us? The Bible says that all angels are ministering spirits sent to serve those who will inherit salvation. How does that happen? How about demons...can they speak? If so, how do they speak? Can they speak from the outside, or only from the inside? How about fallen angels...are fallen angels the same as demons? Do they speak in the same ways as demons?
>
> These questions create the opportunity for a lot of information and response. Just as the Holy Spirit speaks, so do angels, demons, fallen angels, and obviously people, and then of course we have our own thoughts, and our own spirits. If all of these spirits are all talking, it creates that busy intersection I mentioned earlier. It creates Mind Traffic!
>
> If we learn how to control that traffic with authority, just like a police officer in the middle of a busy intersection, then we're going to be able to filter our thoughts and ideas better."

My focus in this chapter is the leading of the Holy Spirit. I also refer to the Holy Spirit as the Spirit of God, or the Spirit of Jesus. God is a triune being, I've learned, and I'm not going to try to prove it in this chapter, but just like people have a body and a soul inside that body that leaves the body when the person dies, there's a part of God that God shares with us in the form of the Holy Spirit. If you want to learn more about other types of spirits, I found Tyler Frick's writings and online seminars very informative and helpful.

Instead of adding more about my theological understanding about the Holy Spirit, I was prompted to share some stories and some illustrations in this chapter from my own life about how sometimes I listened to the wrong voices, and some examples of when I heard God's voice.

One example comes from just a few weeks prior to that sinister moment in my life when I gave into temptation.

My parents had been invited to attend a seminar taught by a couple that had been their marriage counselors for some time. The seminar was on the topic of marriage. My mother asked me to go to the seminar as I was in a relationship at the time that my parents and I thought would eventually lead to marriage.

I believe the gentle voice of the Holy Spirit spoke through my mother when she said, "I think it would be really good if you would go to this marriage seminar, and it may not hurt if you invite your friend also, since you've been seeing each other for a while now and have been thinking about marriage."

Yet the voices in my head said, *I've read so many books already, heard so many sermons on the topic, I know enough, I got this. Besides, that seminar is for mom and dad because they are the ones having marriage problems. Was I not the one who recommended that marriage counseling program? My friend lives all the way in Sacramento. It would be too much to ask. It would be kind of weird. He's probably not interested. He probably has enough understanding as he was recommended by his pastor. He is a leader in his church.* So, I ended up declining that invitation.

Could it be that God wanted to speak to me about my

identity and about how beautiful I was? Could it be He wanted me to know how I was pure in His eyes, and how He will make things work out for my good? Could it be that He may have wanted me to connect with some people during that time, maybe engage in an activity, like translating the workbook (which I ended up attempting to do later on) that may have been helpful to put me in the right framework and mindset in that period in my life? Could it be that He may have given me some ideas of how to navigate through this season of my life in a healthy way, with a healthy mindset?

The morning of that awful temptation, there were thoughts in my mind that were saying, *He's just playing you, you're just one of the girls in his life. Maybe he will never ask you to marry him. Why would he be talking about grad school rather than marriage. And if he doesn't want you, who will want you? You're already pushing 25. You are not that beautiful. He described you as cute. Besides, remember, you're dirty.*

Then, as I was aroused while reading that book, there was a flash thought in my head saying, *If you do this, the consequences will be disastrous,* yet my flesh said, *Go for it, you won't die, you've done it in the past and nothing happened, you're never going to experience real sex anyway. Can't you see? He's got other ideas. You can't trust God to provide a good husband for you, you're dirty. You'll never be good enough.* Why did I not hear God's voice at that time saying, "You are beautiful, you are worth waiting for, you are not defined by your past, your past is covered by my sacrifice"?

Everyone struggles in different ways.

We need to be in constant connection with the Spirit of God so that we can discern when other people are speaking out of their own opinions and judgments, instead of being guided by Holy Spirit.

This does not mean we have to "unfriend" the person, but we can ask God to help us understand what He wants us to hear in a conversation and how we should respond. I wonder how my life would have been impacted if the person that said to me, "You are so stuck up, you only read the Bible and Christian books and pray so you can get people's praise" had said, "I wonder if something happened to you in the past that is making you feel unworthy or insecure about who you are? You know God loves you so much. We feel like we have to do so much for Him to prove ourselves sometimes." What if that person had said later in the week, "I enjoy talking to you, maybe we could talk more sometime"? What if they had become a friend who might have helped me discover the root cause of why I was acting "funny," rather than writing me off and never getting to know me.

It's natural to act from a perspective that is tainted by our past. We see everyone and everything through the lenses of what happened to us. We make assumptions, we withdraw or write people off, and we never really get to know each other. Then, we become superficial and distant in our relationships, and don't even notice when someone is hurting inside or is struggling with some issue. Because we have superficial relationships, we don't develop trust, so we don't open up about our issues; we hide them deep in our subconscious, and we perpetuate the cycle. This dynamic hinders our personal growth, our emotional freedom, and even affects our energy and motivation. We go from being stuck to being more stuck.

I knew so much Bible before the deep dark night of my soul. I had many long chapters memorized. I could look up anything in a heartbeat. I could win a Scripture contest with little effort. I had a deep desire to gain understanding and wisdom. Yet, I had developed a sense of pride in that as well, which really hurt me later. During those dark times, I had to struggle to recite one Bible verse. I could not even pick up the Bible or any other book to read for years.

After I started attending the church community where God began to heal me, I would read a little verse now and then, or people would write down a verse they thought would be helpful for me on a card or a piece of paper and give it to me. I hung on to those verses, and as they kept praying and encouraging me, the Spirit of God kept restoring me gently, little by little.

Now when I read the Bible, it comes so much more alive and meaningful. I struggle to memorize verses word-for-word still, but I know their meaning in my heart, and the Holy Spirit brings them to my memory when I need them. I have a new-found love for the Word of God, and God is showing me beautiful concepts I never understood before.

Now, I hear God's voice saying to me, "You are my beloved daughter, I created you for such a time as this, you are not too old, you are beautiful, and you are loved, and the best is yet to come." It makes a world of difference to know that my identity is not wrapped up in my age, or in my marriage status, or in what others think about me. What matters is what God says, and that makes all the difference. I'm secure in His love and I relate to others from the overflow of His love.

Many things are in competition for attention and our affections.

With the age of electronics, in addition to all kinds of written material, we have TV, cable, internet, and all kinds of social media platforms. It's easy to get lost in the opinions of others, and get confused as to what is real and true, and what ideas are not true and are actually harmful to our well-being. We need Holy Spirit more than ever to help us discern what we should listen to, what we should watch on our devices, and what books and materials we should read in order to guard the affections of our heart. Holy Spirit reminds us to live a disciplined life: to use the time that is gifted to us by God wisely, not just for our own entertainment and enjoyment, but with purpose and to benefit others as well. Personally, spending time with God and spending time with people bring me more joy and fulfillment than anything else. It's good to take a break from all the noise of the media.

I carry my phone everywhere. I use it all the time to check in with my husband and my kids, to check my messages, to answer emails, to write notes, to check on my Facebook groups, to take pictures, to google for information, to enter dates in my calendar, to calculate, and you name it. Once, I was in a hurry to meet for coffee with a friend at a local Starbucks, and I forgot to take my phone. When I realized I forgot my phone, all kinds of thoughts trafficked my mind, *What if my husband needs to call me? What if my kids need me? I can't even check what time it is. What if my friend meant another Starbucks and I'll be waiting for ever and I can't even text her to double check. I had done that just two days before when I went to the wrong Panera Bread for a meeting. Thank God I had my phone for that one and it all worked out as my friend messaged me not to worry and drove to meet me where I was to make it easier for me.*

Just then Holy Spirit reminded me how it used to be when we didn't have cell phones, and how my husband will be okay for a couple of hours if I don't pick up the phone, and how my kids can call him, too, if they need something. I was reminded to pray for a couple of people that have been going through some very hard times lately. It was a sweet time connecting with God without the distraction of my phone and thoughts related to it once I let go. I should do that more often! It turned out that my friend was a few minutes late, but I hardly noticed as I was busy talking to God in my waiting. God is talking to us all the time, but we often can't hear Him because we allow too much noise in our lives.

Jesus taught the disciples to ask God for the Holy Spirit, believing that He is a good Father Who gives good gifts to His children. Jesus indicated that we must be like little children in order to be able to experience the life God intends for us.

When one of our sons was in a private preschool, he had been hearing about how we should pray if we need something because God loves us and listens to us. I was volunteering in his class that day. During playtime, as I was setting up snacks, our sons teacher tapped me on my shoulder and pointed in the direction of my son. My son was gathering his preschool friends saying, "Let's pray that the rain stops, and it will be sunny for recess." Once he rounded up three other friends, they got down on their knees in a circle, and my son asked God for sun for their recess time. They all said, "Amen," and then they got up and went on to play with their toys. It had been raining all morning that day, in fact, it had been raining for days, but when recess time came around, the teacher said to the kids, "Let's look to see if we can go outside for recess today."

As she opened the door, we saw the clouds dispersing quickly just over the school. The rain stopped right before our eyes and the sun shone through. The kids exclaimed,

"Look, we prayed for the rain to stop and God gave us sunshine for recess!" We took the kids to the playground and the clouds stayed in formation all around the school, but over the playground, the kids had the most pleasant time playing in the sun. Then, when recess time was over and the kids got back to class, the clouds and the rain returned immediately. I think God loves to listen to children because they don't reason so much. They just trust that if they ask, God will respond.

I find more and more that God cares so much about us and as we seek His guidance daily, He cares about every little detail of our lives. He cares even about things that we may not even want to ask for because they seem so little and insignificant. I think it's a good idea to ask even for the small stuff because it helps build our faith, so that we can be like little children and believe for the big stuff, too.

Holy Spirit often guides me through my husband.

About 7 years ago I got a report from my doctor about my thyroid, and he said I needed to see a specialist. This time, Holy Spirit prompted my husband to pray and contend for me. My husband got the kids together and they all prayed for me and the thyroid issue the night before driving to Seattle to see the endocrinologist.

The specialist prescribed thyroid replacement hormone medication and said, "You will most likely have to be on it for the rest of your life."

My husband was prompted by Holy Spirit to ask more questions, and the specialist left the room to consult with his team. At that time, my husband and I prayed again and asked God to heal me. When the specialist returned, he said, "Let's do another test just in case, but if the labs come out normal, that would be a bona fide miracle."

After the weekend, we got a call from the specialist saying, "You don't need to take the thyroid medications I prescribed. You can throw them away. Your labs are normal. Your thyroid is fine."

The doctor said one thing, but God had a better answer and a better outcome. I'm glad my husband was with me at that doctor's appointment and heard Holy Spirit on my behalf.

Not long before my own healing, the pastor at the

church we were attending at the time announced that instead of getting in groups that week on Thursday, we were free to listen to the promptings of the Holy Spirit, and reach out to people He brings to mind. When Thursday evening rolled around, we talked about where we should go, as we would normally go to our home group. My husband said, "I feel like we're supposed to visit Diana." She was a client who hired my husband to do some remodeling in her home. She had been diagnosed with cancer and was undergoing naturopathic treatments, as well as chemotherapy. The prognosis did not look good. She had lost fifty pounds, was feeling very weak and discouraged, and to complicate matters, her lungs were affected by the chemotherapy; she was having a hard time breathing and required oxygen.

We visited with her, shared some stories about how God had worked in our lives, and we prayed with her. As we excused ourselves to go home because she said she was not able to tolerate standing for more that a couple of minutes without feeling short of breath, we headed toward the door. Diana was so happy we visited her, and continued to engage us in conversation at the door. We stood there for more than a half hour talking, laughing, sharing more stories about how God was working in our lives, and she did not get out of breath at all. In the days and months to come, Diana shared that she felt better and better. She finished her treatments, and has been cancer free for almost eight years now. She confided in me that she was surprised I had been so vulnerable with her about my personal hellish experience, and that I didn't fear that she may think I'm "crazy." She thought talking with us was helpful, and that God used us to impart the strength and the hope she needed to fight on, along with prayers and support from other people during the hardest times of her life. Now she is full of energy, runs a very busy business, and says it feels like it was all a dream.

Another time Holy Spirit ministered to me through my husband.

My husband reminds me, at times, that women in the early church were encouraged to ask their husbands if they had questions or concerns regarding spiritual matters because Holy Spirit will speak to them through their husbands. Recently, as I was having a hard time concentrating on my work, I had breakthrough when I reached out to my husband. Here's that story as I posted it in one of my Facebook groups:

> "Today I was so blocked in my work. I just could not get myself motivated to finish the paperwork for my consulting business.
>
> I jumped on a prayer call in one of the prayer groups I help facilitate on Zoom just as one of the group leaders was praying specifically for me that the heaviness would be lifted, and the issues I was having with my kids and my husband would be resolved. She had no idea what was happening with me, and she prayed exactly for what I needed before I even said a word.
>
> I felt encouraged by the prayer, but I still had a hard time focusing on my work. Hesitantly, I called my husband and shared with him how I was feeling. He was able to listen and hear my struggle, and he reassured me as we talked about a plan to help resolve my frustrations. Then, he prayed for me, and right away I felt joy and relief.
>
> I resumed my work after the phone call and crushed it in a couple of hours!

Jesus said, when two or three are gathered in His Name, He is there (Matthew 18:20). And He said, when we agree in prayer and ask for something according to His will, we can consider it done (Matthew 18:19)! This was definitely my experience today, and I'm ever so grateful!"

God is good and He enjoys giving good gifts.

As I was asking God to show me what else He wants me to share in this chapter about Holy Spirit, I had this image in my mind of a medium-sized, cheap, flimsy, empty, paper cup that was tipped over. I think God was showing me how sometimes we think God's gifts are like that. As I mentioned earlier, Jesus taught that God gives good gifts to those who ask. His gifts are valuable, like silver and gold, precious treasures that are practical and beneficial for our bodies, souls, and spirits. Things like healing, joy, peace, wisdom, provision, solid and tested truth. He says He did not give us a spirit of fear, but one of power, love and of a sound mind (2 Timothy 1:7). A spirit of a sound mind. Think about it. I encourage you to ask for His Spirit, receive His gift, embrace it, and let Him be the power inside you that inspires you to live a powerful life. A life not just for you, but for all your loved ones and the people you are destined to inspire and empower!

I could go on and on sharing examples, but I think I will stop here and let Holy Spirit lead you as you reflect on what He is saying to you right now. I pray you are able to hear His voice. I would also encourage you to start journaling and writing down your own stories as you experience Holy Spirit guiding you.

Chapter 18 Questions for Reflection:

□ Living a life guided by the Holy Spirit leads to life according to the Bible.

□ What is your understanding of the Holy Spirit?

□ Why is it important to be guided by the Holy Spirit?

□ Are you being guided by the Holy Spirit daily? If not, what can you do about it?

19

FOR PARENTS

My parents did their best to parent me and my siblings. There is no question in my mind that they loved us and provided for us the best way they could. For the most part when they were working, our grandparents cared for us and loved us. They did their best to teach us everything they knew and felt was important for us to learn, and they encouraged us to learn on our own, as well, as we got older. Our parents were very intentional in their parenting.

Still, on the subject of relationships and sexuality, there were things they missed, and at times we ended up being alone with people that should not have been trusted. We were not taught what to do specifically in a situation where someone would approach us inappropriately. There was talk from time to time about sexual integrity, but in very general terms, and it happened after integrity had been already affected negatively. We were not made aware that there would be understanding and possibility for resolution.

Parenting is not easy. There are so many differing theories about how to parent. From my own observations, I believe many parents don't know how to tackle the subject of sexuality with their children. Many parents have not had good models in their own lives. Many parents don't feel comfortable talking about this subject, and avoid it or skim through it, thinking that the kids will eventually figure it out on their own.

At many schools, kids are encouraged to explore their sexuality, and they become sexually active and experiment early on in life, and in the process, are inflicted with extreme emotional pain. Then they are encouraged to see a psychiatrist, where these emotional problems are many times only patched up with medications. The heart issues are inadequately addressed, so the vicious cycle continues. Secular psychiatry does not understand the spiritual implications of sexual relations or deny their existence entirely, and therefore can only address the issues partially. The root cause continues to cause problems.

I want to encourage parents to educate themselves about how to talk with their children about their sexuality through each stage of development. Parents need to learn how to explain what is appropriate and what is inappropriate touch, and what children can do to protect themselves if someone approaches them in a way that is inappropriate. I want to encourage parents to watch their children carefully, to protect them from any potential predators, and to have open communication with them so their hearts may be healed if there has been sexual defilement early on. I want to encourage parents to learn how to communicate at a heart level with their children as they grow and mature. Just telling children what to do and what not to do without providing an adequate foundation can be very damaging.

Parents need to help their children understand the difference between love and lust, and how one protects and the other harms and destroys. Parents need to learn to communicate love in such a way that the young person feels comfortable talking about hard issues without fear of being rejected. As parents, we need to affirm our children's value and worth, and reassure them that there is grace, healing, and restoration if something did happen in the past.

It is so important for parents to really understand how to help their kids navigate in a healthy way through understanding their sexuality. Sexual confusion and frustration can be the start of many, many problems in life, and more and more young people are struggling and are having such a hard time. Many become so overwhelmed that they feel suicide is the only solution.

Everywhere I go, I see people who are deeply hurt by the effects of the so-called freedom of sexual expression. Many are affected by depression, a sense of worthlessness, a gnawing emptiness, and many have no idea what the causes are because of the moral relativism they have grown to accept. I was brought up with very strong moral values and I knew exactly what the cause of my desperation was, and eventually I understood that God had the answer still. I am deeply grateful to my parents for all their efforts to raise me and my siblings well, but with all their best intentions, some things were missed.

When it came to relationships with the opposite sex for me, there was a lack of practical guidance and a lack of specific communication in my young adulthood. There was not a lot of talk about dating or courtship during high school or even college. It was like my parents had an unspoken expectation that we had to finish college and have a career before any of that was even up for discussion.

As a parent, I feel it's crucial that we talk about sexuality and set proper boundaries for dating, as well as make provision for positive experiences within those protective boundaries. You cannot ignore that subject and push it back until after college. There needs to be ongoing communication that starts in childhood. Young people need to be made aware of the importance of sharing with their parents when they have feelings toward someone, and parents and guardians need to know how to guide, encourage and support healthy friendship relationships.

I was talking with a friend not too long ago, and she shared about someone who had many difficulties. She shared about how this person had a new boyfriend, and I asked, "So do they live together?" and my friend immediately responded in anger saying, "Obviously." Later she apologized and said, "I always thought that was just the way it was supposed to be." In today's culture it's even more difficult for a teenager and young adult. With easy access to the internet, young minds are being bombarded with more dangerous and inappropriate information.

Besides creating a loving and supporting environment at home, parents can help their children connect with their age group and form healthy friendship relationships so they can feel secure in the love that flows out of that connectivity. Parents can help by encouraging their children to be active in a healthy church community. One of my pastors and mentors calls this, "keeping their love tank filled." Jesus Christ provides the ultimate fulfillment, but here on earth we need "Jesus with skin on." We need to keep each other's love tanks filled. The body of Christ, the Church, is "Jesus with skin on" here on earth. That is why we need each other so much, and we also need the reality of Christ living in us through the Holy Spirit.

There is a fear of the impossible in the world. Men and women have adopted the mindset that it is impossible to be sexually pure in the culture that we live in, so why even try. I wonder if it would have been different for me knowing what I know now. I kept thinking, *What could I have done differently? How could I have prevented what happened to me?* I have concluded that all my religious training didn't prepare me to deal with the circumstances I faced.

Without a real connection with Jesus Christ and His power my efforts to deal with those circumstances were insufficient. I am so thankful that Jesus redeemed me from my past mistakes. Yet, the lessons that I have learned out of the whole extreme experience are invaluable. I believe that it is possible to change this culture in order that the generations to come may have a better future.

I think one of the reasons why it was so extreme for me was that I was caught in between different cultures. I wanted to do things right, but I was not properly equipped. The pull in this direction and that direction tore me apart. I had partial practical information, and no real understanding as to how to apply what I knew. I pray that God makes a way for me to be helpful to our children and other young people as they navigate through the years ahead in the middle of an ever-changing culture.

I pray that God continues to impart wisdom to me and my husband as parents to help our children navigate through their youth in a healthy way. I pray that churches will become better equipped to train men and women to be true brothers and sisters to each other, providing the love and respect to each other that is so necessary for a healthy life.

When a person feels esteemed, loved, valued, and respected they are more open to receiving instruction, and guidance, so they can keep growing in their strengths and overcome their weaknesses. Churches need to get more equipped and willing to help those who are victims of the current culture. The issues need to be visited often because the lives of our children and future generations are at stake. The church needs to be a place where people find real friendships and real answers rooted in compassion and understanding.

Chapter 19 Summary and Questions for Reflection

If you are a parent, I know you want the best for your kids and you don't want to repeat the mistakes your parents made. It's hard to know how best to parent. I pray that Holy Spirit leads you to parent well and see your children do well!

- ☐ Can you think of some things that may not have been properly addressed in your own upbringing?
- ☐ How can a parent provide adequate protection for their children?
- ☐ How can a parent teach a child to protect themselves?

20

NEVER GIVE UP!

When God completed creation, He said, "And God saw everything that He had made and behold it was very good." I found this book a few years ago written by a Jewish Rabbi, Benjamin Blech, titled, *The Secrets of Hebrew Words*. In his book, under the heading "Adam," he writes:

> "How is it possible that this world, filled as we know it with imperfections, could be declared by the Almighty to be perfect? Is human existence as we know it in fact, טוֹב מְאֹד (*tov me'od*), very good?"[11]

The answer, of course is that it is not good from our perspective if we view history progressively, from Adam through David to the Messiah. But if we were only afforded the vision of hindsight, the retroactive perspective giv-

en to Moses when he asked to behold the glory of God-
"and you shall see My back and My face you shall not see"
– we would finally grasp that everything that appeared
evil when it occurred was part of a far grander and nobler
picture.

It appears the Rabbi implies here that God looked at
what He made and said, "It's perfect." I believe when God
created you, my reader, He said, "Perfect!" He saw you
from the beginning to the end. He saw everything you
were going to experience. He saw the good times and the
excruciatingly difficult times and still said, "Perfect." Then
He says, "For I know the plans I have for you, plans to
prosper you and not to harm you, plans to give you hope
and a future" (Jeremiah 29:11 NIV, paraphrased).

God has a way of guiding us one day at a time. We don't
have a complete picture of what our life is supposed to be
like. We may get an insight today. We may get a glimpse
another day. Some days you may feel like you can't even
crawl out of bed. Some days the darkness is so thick you
can't see two inches in front of you. In those times, I want
to encourage you to hang on. Don't give up! Never give
up! You are worth waiting for! You are gold, no matter
how you are feeling right now, no matter how you failed
or how you feel you don't measure up! God has a good
plan for your life, and though it may take some time, He
will help you get there if you choose to trust Him to do it.

Someone recently messaged me, "I'm trying so hard to
understand." We were chatting about religion. My reply
was, "It's not about **trying**, it's about **trusting**." Try as we
might, we can't ever fully understand God with our mind.
We are limited in our understanding, and God's wisdom
is limitless. We have been given the freedom to choose to
trust Him, to take Him at His word that He will care for us,
no matter what happens, to receive His gift of forgiveness
and restoration through the sacrifice of His Son Jesus, the
perfect sacrifice for our inherited fallen-ness.

Some days you have to choose to trust Him every second. Some days you have to tell yourself every minute that
God has a solution for what happened to you. Some days
you have to tell yourself, *I don't look beautiful to me right
now, but I'm going to trust that He is making me into a mas-
terpiece. He is not finished yet!* Some days you may have to
tell the liar, "I will not believe the lies, I choose to believe

what God says about me." and if you will still your heart and listen, you will hear Jesus say, "I'm here! I love you so much! I invested My life for your good and there's nothing I can't do. You are not too far gone! Trust Me."

Sometimes God may say, "No," to a prayer we pray, or a dream we have. That does not mean His answer will always be, "No." We must exercise patience. We must stay in the game even when we feel all is lost. We can't allow our feelings to have the last word. Our feelings are affected by so many things. Think of your life as a puzzle that God is bringing together. He can see where all the pieces are, and what it will take to get them into their place. He can see all the aspects and He knows all the "Why's." Don't give up on yourself! Never say, "God gave up on me!" God is bigger than your understanding! He is bigger than the thought that is in your mind telling you lies!

During some very difficult times of waiting for me, a friend gave ma a book called, *Pain, Perplexity, and Promotion* written by Bob Sorge. As I read the book, I started to believe that maybe something good could come out of my own sufferings. For a long time, I felt like God singled me out to pick a fight with me, but now I started to understand that there was a bigger picture that was much bigger than me.

On another occasion, I was greeted by a friend at church who said to me, "I just learned that when a caterpillar goes into that cocoon, it liquefies completely on the inside as it transforms into a butterfly." She said, "You are going through a similar transformation." That was quite the picture of what I had been experiencing. Like the caterpillar's insides are dissolved, my inner being was torn, but the picture of a beautiful butterfly emerging at the end of the process inspired me to hang on.

Shortly after the butterfly analogy, I heard Matt Redmond's song, "Blessed Be Your Name." The last bridge of the song says,

> "You give and take away,
> You give and take away.
> My heart will choose to say,
> Blessed be Your Name."[12]

That song spoke volumes to me. It is a choice to praise

God, even when He takes something valuable to me away. It's easy to be thankful and be content when you have everything you want. But something happens when you choose to praise God through the hardest of times, when all you ever held dear is stripped away and all you have left is the choice to still trust God and praise Him.

I chose to praise Him. I chose to sing again, and even to dance. I took a ballet class and learned to dance to the song, "I Surrender All." At the end of the year, each group at the dance academy gave a performance. I was leading two amazing young ladies in the dance, each one weathering through her own life challenges with such sweetness and grace. Before going on stage, I started getting anxious and I started to pray. Then suddenly, I felt like I was a little girl again, and I literally felt Holy Spirit patting me on my right hip like He was saying, "You go, girl." It sent a shiver through me as my body straightened up in confidence. All stage fright left me as I enjoyed every moment of that performance. I felt honored to play a part in encouraging someone in the audience who needed a lift that day, as I had needed a lift from Father God so many times before. And there were tears of joy that day.

There were a few times I said, "never," and later regretted it. Friendships were lost before they could even begin as a result. Opportunities were lost. People were hurt. The truth is, the future is not ours and we should not assume anything about the future. Something that may look like a terrible thing today may turn out to be a blessing tomorrow. As we go through life, our perspectives will change about many things, and it is wise to give ourselves and each other the benefit of believing that we are all being transformed each day by a loving God Who cares infinitely for the world He created. It is wise to forgive ourselves and others even if we have to do it "seventy times seven" times a day and invite God to intervene on our behalf (Mathew 18:22). When we forgive, we create space for God's love to come into our hearts, to heal our hurts, to restore our relationships, and to launch us into a better future than we've ever imagined.

Questions for Reflection:

Do you find yourself facing a situation that seems impossible to solve? What do you do when you are tempted to give up?

What do you think about the statement, "It's not about trying, it's about trusting."

Is there something that you have not shared that may be blocking your progress?

Acknowledgments

What a journey it has been to write and publish this book. Over the years there were so many people that were instrumental in helping me accomplish this task. If I mentioned everyone, the list would be endless, but I am deeply grateful for every person who believed in me and inspired me.

There is one Person I would like to thank first and foremost, one Person Who started it all, Who was there all along even when I thought otherwise, and Who continues to guide me each day. Thank You, Jesus, for all that You are and all that You have done and do for me. Thank You even for allowing all the breaking and thank You for the grace to walk out the story of my life and see the fruit that You produce in and through Your work in me. You are, and always will be, the greatest of Pro's that ever walked the earth and You are my Hero forever.

I want to thank my husband for believing in me and encouraging me to keep writing and to work through the grueling process of editing to bring the book to the finish line. Baby, you have inspired me in so many ways, as we walked through the journey together so far. You have shown me by your example, most of all, as you faithfully go to work every working day, rain or shine, and work through every challenge of re-making a house with patience and perseverance to see it become a place someone can enjoy and call home. You have taught me to not worry so much about what everyone else thinks, and to believe and trust and keep working with what God gave me to bring to the table.

Growing up, it was fascinating to read about and look at various pictures depicting the Seven Wonders of the World, those beautiful ancient creations the Greeks admired so much. Now, I'm fascinated most of all by watching our own seven wonders, our seven children, and I am so grateful for the blessing they are to me and my husband. Each one has been helpful in a unique way as I spent countless hours writing and rewriting. Thank you guys for being so wonderful and so patient with me.

I want to thank my parents, my siblings, and my friends for all your support and encouragement. You have been there through thick and thin.

A big shout out to all my pastors, mentors, coaches, support groups and special thanks to my editors, Naomi, Lynn Ann, Rachel, and those of you who provided feedback for my writings at each level, including Sharon, Ivy, Leslie, Dwight and Peter.

Resources for the Reader

If you are not sure you are in good graces with God, here are some resources for you.

1. Reading the Creator's Manual, the Bible, is my first recommendation. Some say we weren't born with an instruction book. I find the Bible to be quite the instruction book. Statistics say it is the most popular book ever. You may want to start in the New Testament in the gospels (Mathew, Mark, Luke, John) where the four writers describe the birth, life, death, and resurrection of Jesus Christ, the promised Messiah (Savior). It's basically about the story of the love of God. If you read it and don't understand it, it's always good to look for someone who understands it and ask questions about what you're reading, or join a group study.

2. Becoming adopted into the family of God is a simple process of accepting by faith that Jesus is the Son of God, Who came to provide a way to release you from the state of sin you inherited by dying on the cross and carrying the punishment for sin, as the only Person qualified to do so in

the courts of heaven.

Here's a simple prayer you can pray, "Father in heaven, I believe Jesus is your Son, Whom you sent to pay the redemption price for me so that I can live as you have originally created me to live. I ask you to forgive me and receive me into your family. I ask you to come into my heart and guide me as I walk out the life that you have made available for me."

If you prayed that prayer, you may experience a sense of relief right away. Some experience an overwhelming feeling of peace, love, and joy. You may not feel anything at this time. That is okay. Our feelings are affected by many things in life and sometimes our feelings are blocked. There may be things that need to be settled in the courts of heaven before you can experience complete freedom.

As you grow in your understanding of God and His ways, and you start to apply what He teaches you daily, you will start to experience more and more freedom and joy. It's important to keep seeking to know God, to ask lots of questions, and most of all, to learn how to and to practice communicating with God personally and daily. This is possible because God's Spirit comes to live inside your heart to comfort and guide you.

3. If you have many more questions, and are not sure Jesus is the King of Kings, one amazing resource to help you work through your questions is the Alpha Course, which is a group study available in many places around the globe, as well as online. You can find the videos called Alpha Series on YouTube as well. It is always helpful to talk through your questions with someone who understands and is experiencing life as a daughter or son of God.

4. For more resources and support, please visit the author's group on Facebook, "From Power to Power" at www.facebook.com/groups/frompowertopower.

ENDNOTES

1   Graham, Brendan. *You Raise Me Up.* United Kingdom: Decca, 2002.

2   Guyon, Jeanne. *Experiencing the Depths of Jesus Christ* (Library of Spiritual Classics, Volume 2). Jacksonville: Christian Books Publishing House, 1981.

3   https://www.cfaith.com/index.php/article-display/14-articles/23077-quantum-faith

4   Lewis, C.S. *Mere Christianity.* New York: MacMillian, 1952.

5   https://www.desiringgod.org/articles/imitate-me

6   Ibid.

7   https://www.health.harvard.edu/mind-and-mood/in-praise-of-gratitude

8   https://en.wikipedia.org/wiki/Mentorship

9   Warren, Rick. *The Purpose Driven Life: What on earth am I here for.* Grand Rapids: Zondervan, 2002, p. 213.

10   https://pathfindermission.blogspot.com/2013/03/guard-your-heart.html?m=0

11   Blech, Benjamin. *The Secrets of Hebrew Words.* New York: Jason Aronson, Inc., 1996, p.146

12   Redman, Matt & Redman, Beth. *Blessed Be Your Name.* Brentwood: Capitol Christian Music Group, 2002.

About the Author

Daniela Potra is an author who believes in restoring hope, healing, and personal growth after one's darkest moments. She writes poignant stories about surviving deep emotional pain, and shares profound yet practical spiritual truths about overcoming hopelessness.

Her greatest passion is coaching people through mental and physical obstacles towards a fulfilling, purposeful, and abundant life.

Daniela runs a nurse consulting business, and lives in Kirkland, WA and with her husband and seven children.

Made in the USA
Monee, IL
14 August 2021